The Secret Window

HARVARD EAST ASIAN MONOGRAPHS
167

THE SECRET WINDOW

Ideal Worlds in Tanizaki's Fiction

ANTHONY HOOD CHAMBERS

Published by the COUNCIL ON EAST ASIAN STUDIES, HARVARD UNIVERSITY *and distributed by* HARVARD UNIVERSITY PRESS, *Cambridge (Massachusetts) and London* *1994*

Printed in the United States of America

The Council on East Asian Studies at Harvard University publishes a monograph series and, through the Fairbank Center for East Asian Research and the Reischauer Institute of Japanese Studies, administers research projects designed to further scholarly understanding of China, Japan, Korea, Vietnam, Inner Asia, and adjacent areas.

Library of Congress Cataloging in Publication Data

Chambers, Anthony H (Anthony Hood)
The secret window: ideal worlds in Tanizaki's fiction / Anthony Hood Chambers.
p. cm. – (Harvard East Asian monographs ; 167)
Includes bibliographical references and index.
ISBN 0-674-79674-8 : $32.00 (cloth)
1. Tanizaki, Jun'ichirō, 1886–1965—Criticism and interpretation.
I. Series.
PL839.A7Z58 1994
895.6′342—dc20 94-20445
CIP

Index by Julie Perkins

Contents

Preface

This book is a study of seven representative works of fiction by Tanizaki Jun'ichirō.[1] Chapters may be read separately but, since each one builds on those before it, they are best read in sequence. The study assumes some knowledge of the works under discussion, at least in translation.

At the time of his death in 1965 at the age of seventy-nine, Tanizaki had been writing fiction, plays, essays, poems, and translations almost without interruption for more than fifty-five years. He had won every major Japanese literary prize and been decorated by the emperor. His *Complete Works*, including his third modern-Japanese translation of *Genji monogatari* (The Tale of Genji), comprises twenty-eight volumes.[2] After the Second World War he gained international recognition through translations into English and French, and in 1964 he was elected to honorary membership in the American Academy and Institute of Arts and Letters, the first Japanese writer to be so honored. It is widely believed that he would have received the Nobel Prize had he lived a little longer.

Tanizaki's place in the history of Japanese literature seems secure. His novels and stories are sold in almost every bookstore in Japan; many of his works have been adapted for the stage, television, and cinema—even for ballet, opera, and the Bunraku puppet theater. A literary prize is named for him. Films based on his novels have been made in Italy, the Netherlands, and England, as well as in Japan; he has been translated into at least eighteen languages. Gallimard reportedly plans to publish a two-volume collection of Tanizaki in French translation—forty-three stories, novellas, and novels in 4,000 pages. Donald Keene's assessment appears to be coming true: "It is likely that if any one [Japanese] writer of the period will stand the test of time and be accepted as a figure of world stature, it will be Tanizaki."[3]

Tanizaki's prominence in Japanese letters is due partly to his longevity and productivity. He outlived and outwrote most of those whom he considered his rivals. The writers of the Naturalist school, who dominated the Japanese literary world early in the century and delayed Tanizaki's debut by declining to print his stories in the magazines they controlled, faded from the scene early in his career. Proletarian literature flourished briefly but was quashed in the 1930s. The writers of the Shirakaba Group, too, produced little of importance after the 1930s, though two of the most prominent of them—Shiga Naoya (1883–1971) and Mushanokōji Saneatsu (1885–1976)—outlived Tanizaki. The very span of Tanizaki's productive years commands attention. Leo Tolstoy and Mark Twain were alive when he started writing, and his literary debut (with the play *Tanjō* [Birth, 1910]) followed by only five years the debut of the most celebrated Meiji writer, Natsume Sōseki (1867–1916). Tanizaki wrote steadily through the First World War; the prosperity of the 1920s; the depression, nationalism, and militarism of the 1930s; the Second World War; the Allied Occupation and postwar reconstruction; the Korean War; the economic recovery of the 1950s; and the demonstrations of 1960. He was still writing in 1964 when the Shinkansen super-express line began operations, the Olympic Games were held in Tokyo, and the United States involvement in Vietnam deepened.

Each of the seven main chapters in this book focuses on one of Tanizaki's major novels or novellas. A number of aspects are discussed, but the principal concern—introduced in Chapter One—is the attempt by Tanizaki's characters to construct ideal worlds, more or less detached from quotidian concerns, more or less unattainable. A related concern is Tanizaki's fascination with the devices of storytelling, which he uses with great subtlety to evoke his characters' ideal worlds and to encourage the reader's participation in them. Of the works discussed here, only *Sasameyuki* (The Makioka Sisters) fits his description of an "orthodox" or "true" novel, which he defined as one that "is propelled by strictly objective description and dialogue" and that achieves "verisimilitude in characterization and setting through dialogue."[4] The others exploit a variety of less conventional narrative techniques.

Japanese and Chinese names are given in the East Asian style, that is, family name precedes the given name or the pen name. Writers like Tanizaki who have no pen name are generally referred to by the family name, while writers who use a pen name (Nagai *Kafū*, for example) are usually referred to by the pen name. Characters' ages, as well, are given in the East Asian style. The custom is to count the calendar years in which one has lived, rather than the number of full years elapsed since the day of birth.

All translations in the book are my own, unless otherwise noted. Quotations and paraphrases from Tanizaki's writings are identified either in a note or by a reference in the text to the volume and page in *Tanizaki Jun'ichirō zenshū* (28 vols., Chūō Kōronsha, 1966–1968).

Most of this study was completed before Tanizaki Matsuko's death on February 1, 1991, at the age of eighty-seven. Her extraordinary kindness during the twenty years that I knew her enhanced my understanding and enjoyment of her late husband's writings, as well as of kabuki, cuisine, kimono, and many other aspects of Japanese culture, and enriched my life more than I am able to express.

It was the late Professor Ch'en Shou-yi of Pomona College who introduced me to Tanizaki's work. Professor Edward G. Seidensticker supervised my dissertation on Tanizaki, guided my early career, and has continued to be a faithful mentor. I am deeply grateful also to Professor Chiba Shunji of Waseda University, Professor Howard S. Hibbett of Harvard University, and Ms. Ibuki Kazuko, formerly Tanizaki's research assistant and amanuensis. All of them have been wonderfully generous with guidance, encouragement, and friendship.

A Fulbright Scholarship enabled me to begin my research on Tanizaki's writings in 1970–1971. Since then, financial support from the American Philosophical Society, the Associated Kyoto Program, the Japan Foundation, the Mansfield Freeman Center for East Asian Studies at Wesleyan University, and the Wesleyan administration has enabled me to continue my research. I am also indebted to the Reischauer Institute at Harvard University for including me in its programs as an Associate in Research and granting me access to the Harvard-Yenching Library.

Charles Inouye and Ellen Widmer read the entire manuscript at an early stage. Their comments and encouragement came when I needed them most. I am indebted also to the many other teachers and friends who have helped and encouraged me in my research. They include the late Robert H. Brower, Robert B. Campbell, Aileen Gatten, Thomas Hare, Inazawa Hideo, Itō Kunio, William Johnston, Atsuko Kamitakahara, Donald Keene, Paul F. McCarthy, Nakamura Tetsurō, Nguyen Phuong, Okada Satoshi, Onoe Rokujirō, Yoshiko Yokochi Samuel, Takeda Naomi, Ronald A. Takemoto, Tanizaki Shūhei, David A. Titus, Makoto Ueda, Marian Ury, Yamada Sadao, the staff of the International House Library in Tokyo, and the students in my Tanizaki seminars at Wesleyan University, the Associated Kyoto Program, and the Kyoto Center for Japanese Studies. Countless other friends and colleagues have contributed to my understanding of Tanizaki's works, often without realizing that they were doing so. I am profoundly grateful to each of them. I also owe an enormous debt to the many Japanese and Western scholars and critics whose writings on Tanizaki and related subjects have educated, challenged, and inspired me. Finally, none of this study could have been accomplished without the love and encouragement of my parents.

The Secret Window

ONE

Ideal Worlds

Tanizaki included a hidden staircase and a secret window in an upstairs room of the house he designed for himself in Okamoto in 1928. The window disappeared when covered; but when it was open, Tanizaki could gaze into his garden and watch the goings-on, real and imagined, in his private paradise.

The pleasures of reading and writing fiction, for Tanizaki, were "the creation of an imaginary world, and the joys of wandering freely there."[1] He shares these pleasures with his characters and readers: In virtually all of his fiction, Tanizaki has his characters construct and revel in imaginary, alternative worlds, where, because their fantasies are amoral and unfettered by social restraints, they find greater truth, beauty, and pleasure than are available to them in the "real" world with its conventions and rules. Through his manipulation of narrative devices, Tanizaki also induces his readers to participate in these ideal worlds.[2]

The protagonist of the early story *Yanigiyu no jiken* (Incident at Yanagi Bathhouse, 1918) is less subtle than later Tanizaki protagonists but nonetheless representative when he prays, "If you are a dream, . . . let me not wake up! Show me an even stranger, more dreamlike scene! Be a still more fascinating, fabulous dream!" He explains,

> It's human nature to pray that dreams be dispelled, but I'm the opposite. . . . My life is founded on dreams more than on reality. That's why a dream loses no immediacy for me simply because I recognize it

> as a dream. Having a dream gives me real pleasure, just as eating good food and wearing a fine kimono give me pleasure.
>
> (6:131–132)

The protagonist of one of Tanizaki's last works—*Fūten rōjin nikki* (Diary of a Mad Old Man, 1961–1962)—likewise shows a preference for dreams over routine reality. The old man entertains himself with daydreams about his own death, only to be interrupted by his exasperatingly practical wife and daughter. They want to discuss interest payments. An exciting conversation with his daughter-in-law about movies and boxing—handsome men, slippery bodies, violence, blood—is interrupted when his nurse and his wife announce that it's time for his "sliding bed" therapy.[3]

Tanizaki offered a philosophical basis for his faith in imagination in an early essay that reflects his reading of idealist philosophers.[4] "Imagination," he wrote in 1919, is as truthful as "nature."

> Imagination and nature are not essentially so very different. . . . The outer world exists for us only because of our senses. How do hallucinations sketched by the imagination differ from sensations aroused by external stimuli? . . . [A]n artist can scarcely draw the line between hallucinations and natural phenomena. The Naturalist writers esteem experience; but the world of hallucination is no less a part of the experience of an artist who lives in the imagination.
>
> I wonder if "romantic" authors are not those who believe in the possibility of the world of imagination and seek to place it above the world of reality. The artist's intuition leaps over the phenomenal world and sees the eternal world on the other side. This corresponds to the Platonic Ideal—could we not say that a person who tries to live by this creed is a true romanticist?
>
> (22:68–69)

The "hallucinations" in which Tanizaki implicates his characters and readers are neither moral ideals nor models for depraved behavior, but amoral fantasies uncensored by conventional inhibitions and social constraints. His literary politics involve the rejection in fiction (but not, to the degree commonly imagined, in his personal life) of the Confucian ethics inherited by modern Japanese society; of bourgeois preoccupations and conventions; of bureaucrats, politicians, journalists, and militarists; and of respectability, propriety, and everyday aggravations. His fiction and plays capture what we do in our fantasies when we challenge normal reality and social conventions. His works lure the reader into participating in and accepting vivid alternative worlds as preferable to mundane reality. Little wonder the stolid prewar censors considered many of his works "injurious to public morals."[5]

Tanizaki protagonists commonly seek a comfortable, secure world dominated by some version of the Ideal Mother. The quest suggests a desire to return to the security and freedom of uncomplicated childhood, when one is benevolently dominated by Mother and can enjoy the luxury of not having to make decisions or to cope with day-to-day hassles. These worlds apart can be more or less "realistic." *Sasameyuki* (The Makioka Sisters, 1943–1948), for example, offers the reassuring, somewhat idealized world of bourgeois Kansai society before Pearl Harbor. In *Shunkinshō* (A Portrait of Shunkin, 1933), on the other hand, Sasuke seeks a world in which to live in isolation with an ageless, idealized Shunkin. Most of these ideal worlds draw from a common cluster of imagery: water, magical foxes, Mother, music, food, autumn or spring, the full moon, timelessness, and gardens.

Tanizaki's characters employ various means to achieve their worlds apart. Some, like Sasuke, idealize a real woman until the resulting image bears little resemblance to the original.[6] Others try to construct an ideal world around them—or at least do their best with what is available.[7] All of them encounter obstacles: time and change (in the case of *Ashikari* [The Reed Cutter, 1932], *A Portrait of Shunkin, The Makioka Sisters,* and *Yume no ukihashi* [The (Floating) Bridge of Dreams, 1959]); distance and inaccessibility (*Yoshino kuzu* [Arrowroot, 1931], *Bushūkō hiwa* [The Secret History of the Lord of Musashi, 1932–1935], and *Shōshō Shigemoto no haha* [Captain Shigemoto's Mother, 1949–1950]); and, in every case, intrusions from the external, "real" world.

The reader's wanderings in these imaginary worlds are given scope by the narrative shadows that Tanizaki advocated and employed. "In the mansion called literature," he writes in his most famous essay, "I would have the eaves deep and the walls dark, I would push back into the shadows the things that come forward too clearly, I would strip away the useless decoration."[8] Tanizaki's shadows are full of ideas and hints. The darkness of his prose, like that in the Sumiya teahouse in Kyoto, is "a repletion, a pregnancy of tiny particles like fine ashes, each particle luminous as a rainbow."[9] The reader is subtly guided through the suggestive darkness by narrators who employ complex narrative manipulations to steer the reader in this direction or that. The reader's freedom to wander is, then, ultimately an illusion. Some readers of Tanizaki surrender happily; others may resent the manipulations.

Ideal worlds are conspicuous in all periods of Tanizaki's career. This study focuses particularly on seven novels and novellas from his middle and late years, beginning with *Arrowroot* (1931), a novella that is both representative of Tanizaki's fiction and a watershed in his career.[10] Nineteen-thirty, the year in which Tanizaki published his first "Complete Works," divorced his first wife, and wrote *Arrowroot,* marks a turning point in both his personal life and his literary style.[11] Though it attracted little attention at first, *Arrowroot* heads Satō Haruo's list of Tanizaki masterpieces. *Arrowroot, Mōmoku monogatari* (A Blind Man's Tale, 1931), and *A Portrait of Shunkin* were so superior, Satō wrote, that he would have had no regrets if all of Tanizaki's pre-*Arrowroot* writings disappeared.[12] *Arrowroot* represents an abrupt change in Tanizaki's writing: it is the work of a mature writer who has put aside the defiant, pretentiously Westernized, hedonistic masquerade of most of the earlier works; and it anticipates much of what was to come.[13]

of a nō play: the *waki* usually appears on stage first and fixes the attention of the audience, but his main function is to set the scene for the *shite*, provide a foil for him, and encourage him to tell his story.[7] As the focus of *Arrowroot* shifts and narrows, the central question turns out to be, "Then what is the purpose of this trip?," as the narrator asks Tsumura at the beginning of the last chapter, fulfilling his role as *waki* by eliciting the heart of the story from the *shite*. Tsumura, about to unveil his last secret, replies, "Well, there is something I haven't told you about yet" (192).

In addition to the *waki-shite* relationship, *Arrowroot* adapts the *jo*, *ha*, and *kyū* (introduction, agitated development, quick close) structure and rhythm of the nō and other genres of Japanese performing arts. In a representative nō play, the *waki* makes his entrance in the *jo* and explains why he has come to the site of the drama. The *shite* enters during the first part of the *ha* and hints of his past in an emotional narration. In the second section of the *ha*, the *waki* and the *shite* discuss the history of the site; and in the third section of the *ha*, the *shite* relates past events at the location. The pace gradually quickens as the play moves from one section to another.[8] These divisions correspond with Tanizaki's chapters. The *jo* consists of the narrator's commentary on the Heavenly King and his decision to accompany Tsumura to Yoshino in "The Heavenly King." The *ha* begins with the travel account that takes the two men from Nara to Natsumi in "Imoseyama." This lyrical chapter, studded with literary allusions, is a *michiyuki*—a poetic litany, common in Japanese theater, of the sights and impressions of a journey. The *michiyuki* helps suspend disbelief by lulling the reader into a world apart—from the immediate, everyday world of Tokyo, via the old capitals of Kyoto and Nara, to a timeless setting in the depths of the Yoshino mountains, a dream world where Tsumura can establish his own "reality" and unfold his mystery to increasingly receptive narrator and readers. The *ha* continues with the visit to the Ōtani house in "The Drum Hatsune" and Tsumura's disclosures in "The Cry of the Fox" and "Kuzu." In the *kyū*, "Shionoha," the narrator and Tsumura go to Kuzu together, the narrator hikes into the mountains, and finally the narrator is reunited with Tsumura and Owasa.

The narration flows from the secondary narrator (Tsumura), to the primary narrator, and finally to the reader. This degree of distancing is particularly effective in creating the narrative "shadows" that Tanizaki advocated, because the action is far enough removed to afford the reader's imagination room to grow. The shadows are deepened by the chronology: the narrator is recalling a trip already twenty years in the past, and Tsumura's reminiscences go back another twenty years. Chronological distancing also enhances the story's plausibility, as Itō Sei has pointed out: "The narrative begins with the actuality of the narrator—in other words, with the present—and works gradually back into the past. In the process, the sense of present reality is extended to a sense of reality in the tale of the past. It is the technique of a picture scroll that begins with the present and moves back in time as it is unrolled."[9]

Tsumura's search for his mother's village is ordinary enough; but by placing it in rich geographical, historical, legendary, and literary contexts, Tsumura endows it with a splendor and universality that induce the narrator and the reader to participate in his world with him. Even a reader who is not already familiar with Yoshino lore will recognize the fundamental appeal of spring blossoms and autumn foliage; an ancient, exciting history; folkloric archetypes, such as "mysterious mountain recesses," "the sacred jewel hidden deep in a cave" (148), and magical foxes; and, above all, a child's quest for his lost mother. Tsumura universalizes his story by cloaking it in these elements. The village of Kuzu becomes the prototype of all hometowns lost or forgotten in the rush of modernization; Tsumura's search for his mother embodies longings that everyone feels.

The associations that bring a setting alive are abundant in Yoshino. Recalling *Arrowroot* thirty-two years after its publication, Tanizaki contrasted Tokyo (the narrator's home) with Yoshino:

> Cherry-blossom viewing in Tokyo is simply a matter of sitting in a tea room behind bamboo screens, eating dumplings, roast taro, and hard-boiled eggs, and drinking bottled Masamune. In the shadow of these flowers are no Yoshitsune, Wakaba-no-Naishi, Shizuka, Tadanobu, or Genkurō the fox, no Hatsune drum or Hiodoshi armor. Blossom viewing without these associations did not seem to me like blossom viewing at all. . . . There is no fantasy in the Tokyo blossoms. But when I went to see the famous blossom sites in western Japan I felt as

> though I might somewhere meet the phantom of Wakaba-no-Naishi or Lady Shizuka, and at times I even felt as if I had turned into a fox or into Gonta and was wandering about, lured [as on the stage] by the sound of a drum or a whistle.
>
> (19:458)

References to the history of the Southern Court and the legendary Heavenly King dominate the introductory section of *Arrowroot.* The narrator mentions the nō play *Kuzu* and the fourteenth-century chronicle *Taiheiki* and lists the books he has used in his research.[10] The most important associations in the rest of the novella are with fox legends in the plays *Yoshitsune senbonzakura* (Yoshitsune and the Thousand Cherry Trees) and *Arrowroot Leaves,* and in the song *Konkai* (The Cry of the Fox).

The relatively short *michiyuki,* which follows the introductory section, is particularly rich in allusions. The most important allusion is to the fox Genkurō (a character in *The Thousand Cherry Trees*), who is drawn to Minamoto Yoshitsune's mistress Shizuka and to her drum Hatsune, because his parents' skins have been used to make it. The subject of the fox and the drum is broached gradually. When Tsumura first mentions *The Thousand Cherry Trees* and Hatsune, the narrator pulls the narrative back to a factual, concrete level by quoting from the nō play *Futari Shizuka* (The Two Shizukas) and *Yamato meisho zue* (Famous Places in Yamato, Illustrated), and then only cautiously refers to Yoshitsune and Shizuka. The effect is to pace the emergence both of Tsumura as the central character and of the principal theme of the novella.[11]

In the exposition section, extended allusions to *The Thousand Cherry Trees,* the fox Genkurō, *Arrowroot Leaves,* and *The Cry of the Fox* bring the fox theme to the center of attention. There is also an allusion to a celebrated ninth-century love poem:

> Satsuki matsu hanatachibana no ka o kageba
> mukashi no hito no sode no ka zo suru
>
> The orange blossoms that wait for early summer
> Bear the fragrance of the sleeves of the one of old.
>
> (*Kokinshū* no. 139, anonymous)

This is the only allusion in the novella that is unrelated to Yoshino, which suggests that Tanizaki chose it especially for its thematic relevance. The allusion comes when Tsumura is thinking about his mother, and so contributes to a theme that has been developing with the fox allusions—that Tsumura's filial longing for his mother is also a romantic longing.

The Genkurō-Shizuka story has special significance for Tsumura because he believes that there are romantic overtones in the relationship between the fox and Shizuka. This is not as far-fetched as its sounds. Though the fox (in the form of Yoshitsune's retainer Tadanobu) and Lady Shizuka are in a servant-master relationship, the *michiyuki* of *The Thousand Cherry Trees* is choreographed to look like a lovers' journey. Tanizaki elaborated on this idea many years later:

> Since it is the hand of a beautiful woman that holds the drum, there is no feeling of cruelty. Indeed, the child fox might well feel anger at the heartlessness of human beings; but if I, with my masochistic inclinations, were that child fox, I would on the contrary feel all the more affection for Shizuka and wish to serve her the more loyally.
>
> (19:453)[12]

According to Tsumura's interpretation, then, Genkurō the fox is romantically attracted to Shizuka because he associates Shizuka with the longing he feels for his mother; and the fox's situation becomes a metaphor for Tsumura's own. In his mind the concepts of "mother," "fox," "beautiful woman," and "lover" are intimately associated. In this context, Tsumura describes an aspect of his psychology that is frequently encountered in Tanizaki's male characters:

> I am convinced that, from the first time I heard the song [*The Cry of the Fox*], my imagination saw more than just my mother. The figure I saw was my mother, I think, and at the same time, my wife. And so the image of my mother that I held in my little breast was not that of a matron, but that of an eternally young and beautiful woman.
>
> (175–176)

One could hardly ask for a clearer statement of the fantasy that Tsumura shares with other Tanizaki men. The man is both child and husband; the woman, both mother and lover. As Tsumura says of *Arrow-*

root Leaves, "the father and the son are of one mind in their love for the mother" (176).

It is not quite enough, however, for Tsumura to put his longings in a universal context. Before the narrator can identify with them, he must set aside the modern rationality of a deracinated Tokyo writer and learn to appreciate legends and fantasies.[13] He is more than just a *waki,* because his growing sensitivity is a central theme of *Arrowroot.*

At first the narrator sees no need to go to Yoshino at all: "I had completed my research on everything that could be investigated from a distance, and if Tsumura had not prodded me, I surely would never have set out for those mountain recesses. I had so much material that my imagination would take care of the rest, even without a visit to the site. In fact there are certain advantages to proceeding that way" (151). Tsumura, on the other hand, stresses that there is more to Yoshino that the history of the Southern Court.

The narrator's attitude begins to change as soon as he reaches the Yoshino River. Gazing upstream from the bridge at Mutsuda toward Imoseyama (and toward Tsumura's ancestral village), he remembers having seen this view before as a child, his mother holding him, "young and impressionable, on her lap" and whispering in his ear. Visiting Yoshino again in his youth, he "leaned once more on the bridge railing and thought of my dead mother as I gazed upstream" (153–154). A less romantic type than Tsumura, he has not dwelled on memories of his mother, but they have reasserted themselves nonetheless "at unexpected times," when he has recalled the view from the bridge "with a pang of nostalgia." In hiking upstream with Tsumura, then, the narrator, too, is pursuing memories of his mother, perhaps without realizing it.

Presently the narrator reverts to the skeptic. When Tsumura mentions *The Thousand Cherry Trees,* the narrator thinks of Koremori and the famous Tsurube sushi-shop scene, which he dismisses as fiction, despite its importance to the residents of Shimoichi. Tsumura is more interested in the scenes that involve Shizuka's drum Hatsune than he is in the sushi scene, and he wants to visit a family in Natsumi that claims to possess the drum. Again the narrator is skeptical, even pedantic: There is no historical evidence that Shizuka was ever in Yoshino, he says, and the forebears of the Ōtani family were probably inspired by

The Two Shizukas (which is set in Natsumi) to identify their drum as Shizuka's. As it turns out, the narrator is right—the drum appears not to be authentic. But Tsumura is undeterred. He is interested not in the literal facts, but in the idea—the tradition, the fantasy, the mystery—of Shizuka and the fox.

The Ōtani family also has a scroll that purports to be a history of Natsumi, but it, too, is dubious. Rather than helping to establish the true history of the region, the clumsy document ironically serves to remind the narrator of the importance of tradition and symbolism. The head of the Ōtani family believes that Shizuka left her drum there, and he believes in the scroll. The "truth" does not matter—the drum and the scroll symbolize the past glory of his family; they are the focal points of his respect for the past and they help him to find meaning in the present. Thus the narrator's faith in historical "fact" and his skepticism of tradition are weakened. History, as Tsumura has told him, is not everything; dreams about the past are important.

The journey up the river is a sensory delight. The narrator, accustomed to finding stimulation in books, finds it here in the "cold white" paper on the shōji, the "glossy, ripe coral surfaces" of persimmons glowing in the afternoon sun, the "sounds of a blacksmith's hammer and the *sah-sah* of a rice polisher" (155–156), and especially in the ripe persimmons that he eats at the Ōtani house. Ultimately it is the persimmons that make the deepest impression on the narrator—"I filled my mouth with the Yoshino autumn," he recalls (166). In their rich vitality, they embody the non-cerebral world that he is learning to appreciate. Savoring Yoshino with all of his senses has reawakened this bookish writer, estranged in Tokyo from the Japanese heartland, to the roots of his culture. He is ready now to listen to Tsumura's story.

Tsumura has clung to his dreams even when the facts justify skepticism. He has no clear memories of his mother but cherishes a vague image of her playing *The Cry of the Fox* on the koto. It does not matter that it was probably his grandmother, not his mother, whom he remembers. When he is shown a koto that belonged to his mother, the instrument excites his imagination, even though it may not be the koto he remembers. It is the fantasy that the koto stimulates that is important, not the precise identity of the koto or of the woman whom he remembers playing it. Similarly, Tsumura's fox-mother fantasies are stimulated by the discovery that his maternal grandfather actually worshipped a fox—a real fox—that lived near his house in Kuzu; but there is no fox when Tsumura arrives in Kuzu. Even Aunt Orito remembers little. She may even have forgotten her sister's name. The visit to Kuzu, in short, produces hardly any concrete information about Tsumura's mother: there is no fox, the koto is questionable, Orito's memory is unreliable. But none of this matters to Tsumura. On the contrary, the absence of facts is fuel for his fantasies.

Near the end of the novella the narrator sets out one last time in pursuit of facts, but his expedition deep into the Yoshino mountains beyond the village of Kuzu produces only fatigue and disappointment. He finds it impossible to learn the truth about the Heavenly King, despite his original confidence, and abandons his project. "Sannoko may be the site of legends," he concludes, "but not of history" (198). As the narrator emerges from the mountains, leaving history behind, he sees Tsumura and Owasa crossing toward him on a suspension bridge. "The bridge swayed slightly under their weight and the sound [*ko-n, ko-n*] of their wooden sandals echoed in the valley" (198–199). In Japanese convention, "*ko-n, ko-n*" is the sound of the fox's bark. With this haunting image, at once visual, aural, and romantic, the fox formerly venerated by Tsumura's grandfather comes back to life in the person of Tsumura's rediscovered "fox-mother," Owasa. Just as the persimmons upstage history and the senses eclipse the intellect, Tsumura's fantasies culminate in a marriage of archetypal happiness, while the narrator's research comes to nothing, except the story he has told.

THREE

The Secret History of the Lord of Musashi

A few months after completing *Arrowroot,* Tanizaki went on a working honeymoon with his second wife to the Shingon Buddhist complex on Mount Kōya. There he began writing *The Secret History of the Lord of Musashi,* the most eccentric of his major works. He also studied esoteric Buddhism and completed the novella *A Blind Man's Tale* while he was there.

A Blind Man's Tale and *The Secret History of the Lord of Musashi* are both set in the second half of the sixteenth century, an age of warfare among rival daimyō, and both purport to reveal a secret underside of history; but in tone they could hardly be more different. *A Blind Man's Tale* is a fictional masseur's personal narrative about his life in service to Lady Oichi; the center of interest is his unusual perspective on well-known historical events and persons. The tone is meditative and understated, in keeping with the masseur's reverence for Oichi and the highly deferential language in which he tells his story.[1] The ironic tone of *The Secret History*, on the other hand, is appropriate to the magazine that solicited it. Tanizaki published *A Blind Man's Tale* in the high-brow *Chūō Kōron,* but serialized *The Secret History* in *Shinseinen* (New Youth), which specialized in fantasies, satires, cartoons, Western fiction in translation, and, above all, mysteries. Its most important regular contributor was Edogawa Ranpo (1894–1965), who had contrived his pen name to sound like "Edgar Allan Poe." *Shinseinen,* slick and sophisticated, was read by intellectuals looking for diversion.[2]

Tanizaki characterized *The Secret History* as "popular fiction" and apparently wrote it in hopes of improving his finances. In a letter dated July 4, 1931, he says (after describing his financial problems), "I had decided not to write any more popular fiction [*tsūzoku mono*], but now I am thinking of writing just one more to raise some money."[3] Tanizaki's interest in "popular fiction" was deeper than this comment suggests, however. He had already written the wildly imaginative *Rangiku monogatari* (A Tale of Chrysanthemums in Chaos, 1930) and championed popular, imaginative literature in several essays.

"Popular literature" had its beginnings in the burgeoning circulation of the great daily newspapers in the mid-1920s. It was convenient for Tanizaki, residing in Kansai after the earthquake, that the biggest newspapers—the *Asahi* and the *Mainichi*—were based in Osaka. "Each passed a million in nationwide circulation the year after the earthquake. The largest Tokyo newspaper had a third of a million."[4] To please their relatively sophisticated readers, these papers required "absorbing, but not too lowbrow" pieces of fiction.[5] Tanizaki praised Nakazato Kaizan's mammoth romance *Daibosatsu Tōge* (Daibosatsu Pass, 1913–1935) and wrote that the "popular" works of the time, particularly historical fiction, were more to his taste than the confessional writings of the Naturalists, the Shirakaba writers, and their successors, or the products of the proletarian literary movement (20:73–80). In the same year (1926), he wrote:

> I have acquired a bad habit recently. I cannot bring myself to write or read anything that takes real facts for its material, or that is even realistic. This is one reason I make no attempt to read the works of contemporary authors that appear in the magazines every month. I scan the first five or six lines, say to myself, "Aha! he's writing about himself," and lose all desire to go on reading. . . . I have come to prefer perversity to simplicity, sophistication to artlessness. . . .
>
> Generally I read things that have nothing to do with the present. When I read historical novels, nonsense tales, even realistic novels of fifty years ago, or contemporary Western novels far removed from Japanese society, I can enjoy them as so many imaginary worlds. Last year I read a number of historical novels. I was most impressed with Nakazato Kaizan's *Daibosatsu Pass*, *Héloise and Abélard* and *Ulick and Soracha* by George Moore, and *The Charterhouse of Parma*, "The Abbess of Castro," and one or two others by Stendhal.
>
> (20:72–73)[6]

Later he went so far as to suggest that "popular" writers were closer to the main stream than the writers of "pure" literature:

> Confessional and "state of consciousness" novels may be considered highclass, but they certainly do not represent the main stream of the novel. The essential nature of the novel is that it appeal to the general public and that it have a definite structure and conscious artistry, like the fiction of the Tokugawa period. The fact is that in most cases works of this sort require greater technical skill and discipline than the so-called high-class pieces, and cannot be dashed off by someone who lacks experience and preparation.
>
> (22:290–291)

Tanizaki wrote this in May, 1930, while he was at work on *Chrysanthemums in Chaos,* an historical fantasy he described as "popular." Given free rein in this format, Tanizaki's imagination ranged from ghosts, avatars, and imaginary lands to the treasure-hunt motif—elements that are often found in Tokugawa-period *yomihon* (the works of Takizawa Bakin [1767–1848], for example) but would have been considered out of place in modern pure literature. In the late 1920s Tanizaki had expressed an ambition to write a long historical novel comparable to Henryk Sienkiewicz's *Quo Vadis,* set in the Kamakura or Ashikaga period, with courtiers, shōgun, priests, and ladies involved in complex relationships (20:476). *Chrysanthemums in Chaos,* which is set in the Ashikaga period, may be a partial fruition of this ambition. Tanizaki left it unfinished, apparently interrupted by the events leading up to his divorce in August, 1930, and then by his desire to complete *Arrowroot;* but he was thinking about a sequel as late as 1960.[7]

Another perspective on the beginnings of *The Secret History* is provided by an announcement in the July, 1931 issue of *Shinseinen:* "Mr. Tanizaki Jun'ichirō has agreed to write a full-length novel for this magazine. Serialization will begin with the September issue. . . . This is a work he has been planning for a long time."[8] While Tanizaki's July 4 letter gives the impression that writing *The Secret History* was a whim of the moment, the editor's announcement, together with the richness and complexity of the work itself and Tanizaki's determination to write a sequel, give the opposite impression—that he had given much thought to the work and was deeply committed to it.

For all that, Tanizaki never completed *The Secret History* in the form he envisioned. In a letter to his editor enclosed with the October, 1932 installment, he wrote:

> *The Secret History* has reached only the midpoint of my plan; ultimately it will be at least twice as long as what I have written so far. With your approval, however, I would like to break it off after another three or four installments, and then start afresh on a sequel. My ambition is to make this a truly fine work, and so I shall certainly write the sequel. If this is inconvenient for you, I would not mind contracting with another magazine. Please give it some thought. In any case, I do not think that one or two more installments will be enough to reach the most interesting part—the essential point I aim for. I would like to write that far and then bring the first volume to a close at an appropriate spot.[9]

The last published installment, in the November, 1932 issue of *Shinseinen,* includes the conclusion of the chapter "In Which Ojika Castle Falls, and Norishige is Taken Prisoner," and the beginning of a new chapter, "In Which a Barricade Prevents Supplies from Reaching Sabae Castle, and the Occupants Eat Whatever They Can Find." The February, 1933 issue of *Shinseinen* carried Tanizaki's explanation to his readers:

> On the continuation of *The Secret History of the Lord of Musashi*
>
> *The Secret History of the Lord of Musashi*, which you have been kind enough to read all these months, is of course not complete with the final installment of last year. I began to write, however, with the agreement that the novel would be serialized for one year, and I expected to be able to complete it in that time; but the story unfolded more slowly than I had anticipated, and in twelve installments I wrote only half of what I had planned. I have commitments to other magazines now, but in about six months, when my other work is completed, I intend to write the sequel to this novel. At that time I will rewrite from the opening of the last chapter, "In Which a Barricade Prevents Supplies from Reaching Sabae Castle, and the Occupants Eat Whatever They Can Find." This is a tale that I have been planning for a long time and shall certainly not leave unfinished.[10]

The same issue carries an announcement that serialization of *The Secret History* would resume in the summer of that year; similar announcements appear in the August and October issues. It is clear that both the author and the editors planned on a sequel to follow shortly. The sequel was never written. Instead, Tanizaki pulled the installments together and published them, somewhat revised, in book form in 1935. The word *kan* ("complete") on the title page indicates that the novel was to be considered a finished work.[11]

In his revisions, Tanizaki dropped the fragmentary "Sabae Castle" chapter and provided a new ending for what became the last chapter, "In Which . . . Norishige is Taken Prisoner." He also shortened the "Preface" and recast it from modern Japanese into classical Chinese, grouped the chapters into books (*maki*), and made a number of cuts. Some of the revisions made *The Secret History* look more like certain premodern Japanese genres. The Chinese preface, for example, has precedents in any number of premodern works.[12] The chapter headings of *The Secret History* also have an antique look. Such titles as "Tsukuma Norishige mitsukuchi ni naru koto, narabi ni jōrō no kawaya no koto" (In Which Tsukuma Norishige Acquires a Harelip, and the Toilets of High-ranking Ladies are Described) follow the pattern established by *setsuwa* collections, chronicles, *ukiyozōshi*, and such *yomihon* as Bakin's *Chinsetsu yumiharizuki* (Crescent Moon, 1807–1811).

Tanizaki cut some passages because they anticipated events that the uncompleted narrative never reached. The following paragraph, for example, originally appeared toward the end of the chapter "In Which Dōami Sheds Tears of Gratitude, and Shōsetsuin Grieves," after Terukatsu has tried to convert his wife into a companion for his sadistic "games":

> For Terukatsu, a captive of his own "shameful," perverse lust, this incident was the first conscious, deliberate step toward depravity. . . . During his life, many innocent women suffered wretched fates because of the Lord of Musashi, their lives cut short and their reputations blemished, and of these Shōsetsuin was the first. This is the first page in the bizarre history of Terukatsu's sexual desires that will unfold from here on; and it is here that the sufferings of his conscience begin.[13]

This passage had to go, because in the 1935 revision of *The Secret History* Shōsetsuin is not only the first, but also the last such woman.

Several passages that survived the revisions hint at developments more frightening and more final than anything included in the work as we have it. The "Preface" points out, for example, that Fukushima Masanori's sexual life led to his downfall (3).[14] A few pages later, the narrator anticipates the course of Terukatsu's career when he says that "few of the men and women who participated in the lord's 'games' escaped with their lives" (9), but the events hinted at are never fleshed out. Similarly, nothing in the novel accounts for Terukatsu's appearance: "the lord's countenance betrays a touching look of anguish, and the figure of the brave, armor-clad warrior comes to resemble a prisoner moaning grimly in the stocks" (11).

Tanizaki's desire to write a sequel to *The Secret History* did not fade with time. In 1948 and 1949, when he negotiated with the *Mainichi Shimbun* for the serialization of a new novel, he planned to write the sequel but ultimately wrote *Shōshō Shigemoto no haha* (Captain Shigemoto's Mother) instead.[15] An unpublished notebook that apparently dates from 1949 contains an outline of the 1935 version of *The Secret History*, including the names of places and characters, dates, and events, all followed by numbers, and such entries as "The Lord of Musashi's psychology—206." The numbers coincide with page numbers in the 1935 edition. In short, Tanizaki reread the novel in 1949 and took notes on the names and dates he would need to remember as he wrote the sequel. At the end of the notes he set down a title in bold characters: "Naburi monogatari: zoku Bushūkō hiwa" (A Tale of Bullying: The Secret History of the Lord of Musashi, Continued). Presumably he meant to outline his sequel in the empty pages that follow.

The degree of Tanizaki's interest in the sequel is attested to by his former research assistant and amanuensis, Ibuki Kazuko:

> I believe that the sequel to *The Secret History* is something that Mr. Tanizaki truly wanted to write. At times he was impatient and quick to tire of a project; frequently he would make up his mind to write something, only to conclude, as he was gathering material or thinking it out, that it was not worth writing after all, or that there might be trouble of some kind. At such times he would drop a project without a second thought. . . . He was most eager about the sequel to *The Secret History*. I never heard him say that he had given it up. I do remember him saying, "I wanted to write the sequel as soon as I'd

> finished the first part." I believe it was in 1960 or 1961 that he was most enthusiastic about it.[16]

According to an unpublished outline prepared by Tanizaki in 1960, both Dōami and Terukatsu were to suffer castration in the sequel.[17] Even without knowing of Tanizaki's plans, many readers have no doubt sensed that the concern with severed heads, and especially with noseless ones, has something to do with castration. To one who does know, the early descriptions of Terukatsu—"a touching look of anguish," "a prisoner moaning grimly in the stocks"—sound like anticipations of the fate Tanizaki had planned for him. The underlying image of castration is present even in the revised, 1935 version of *The Secret History.* The nose is described in phallic terms—"one would expect to find a sculpturesque protuberance soaring from the middle of this splendid face," so that the absence of "that vital feature" suggests castration (32–33). There is also a clear hint that both Terukatsu and the narrator associate the nose with castration:

> It seems highly doubtful that the object he presented to her as "a memento of Lord Masataka" at their first meeting was actually a relic of Yakushiji Danjō Masataka at all. . . . Terukatsu probably cut a nose from one of the corpses that lay scattered nearby and used it as a tool to excite Lady Kikyō's hostility. . . . In fact, since he had preserved it in red ink, it need not have been a nose at all: any soft lump of roughly the same shape would have sufficed. But it would be indelicate to speculate any further on what the object in the jar might have been.
>
> (84)[18]

The obsession that drives the Lord of Musashi is, then, a castration fantasy. As it begins to take shape, he identifies himself with a severed head being prepared for display—a head with nose intact:

> Hōshimaru envied the head placed before the beautiful girl. He was jealous. But it is important to understand the nature of this jealousy. It is not simply that he envied the head for having the girl dress its hair, shave its pate, or gaze at it with that cruel smile; he wanted to be killed, transformed into a ghastly head with an agonized expression, and manipulated in the girl's hands. Becoming a severed head was a

> necessary condition. He found no pleasure in imagining himself alive at her side; but if he could become such a head and be set before her in all her charm, how happy he would be!
>
> (30)

This is not a fantasy he chooses. It puzzles and frightens him, and he has no control over it; and yet it gives him intense pleasure:

> He indulged in the fancy that he had become a head without losing consciousness. He tried to imagine that one of the heads brought before the women was his own. When the girl tapped a head with the ridge of her comb, he imagined that he himself was being tapped, and this brought his pleasure to the very summit: his brain grew numb and his body trembled.
>
> (31)

The fantasy takes on a sharper focus when he sees a noseless head—a "womanhead"—for the first time:

> He thought he would never tire of gazing at her smiling face. The fantasies it inspired were inexhaustible and, before he was aware of it, had lured his soul away to a land of ambrosial dreams where he himself had become this noseless head and was living with the girl in a world inhabited only by the two of them. This fantasy was very much to his liking. It made him happier than he had ever been before.
>
> (33)

Terukatsu's compulsion to enact this dream becomes the driving force of his life and ultimately leads (in the sequel outline) to his castration.[19]

Though he is obsessed by a castration fantasy, Terukatsu does not deliberately seek to be castrated. "At times," the narrator says, "he would become too engrossed and be lured to the brink of disaster, but he never forgot to draw himself up short of the last step" (84). If he were to be castrated at the end of the sequel, it would be because he lost his balance on the "brink of disaster." A story Tanizaki published a few years earlier, "Nihon ni okeru Kurippun jiken" (A Crippen Affair in Japan, 1927), sheds light on this aspect of masochist psychology as Tanizaki understood it:

> [A] masochist does not become a woman's slave; he enjoys appearing to be one. He would be annoyed if she made him a real slave. Maso-

chists are, then, egoists. Though they may sometimes carry their acts too far and die by mistake, they never give their lives up willingly, like martyrs, to a woman.

(11:33)

Other clues appear in *The Secret History:* "Masochistic pleasure is, after all, a form of pleasure, and so it clearly involves an element of self-interest" (83). In pursing his self-interest, the masochist often looks like a sadist as he toys with people around him to achieve his masochistic ends. Thus "[a] man who has masochistic sexual appetites . . . is apt to construct fantasies in which his female partner conforms to his own perverse specifications; and so the woman, in most cases, is not at all the pitiless creature she is made out to be" (63).

The cruelty and sado-masochism in *The Secret History* recall the neighborhood *chaban* productions that provided Tanizaki with "weird and ghastly dreams" in his childhood.[20] They also recall the kabuki theater. Writing on *The Secret History,* Masamune Hakuchō is reminded of a kabuki print in which a man, looking pleased with himself, has a woman pour saké for him while he gazes at another man bound to a column, an unsheathed sword thrust into the matting before his nose.[21] It is not far from a scene like this, common enough in kabuki, to the passage where Terukatsu and his wife drink together as they watch Dōami play the part of a severed head.

Tanizaki acknowledged the influence of his favorite kabuki play, *Yoshitsune and the Thousand Cherry Trees,* on *The Secret History.* The narrator compares Terukatsu's first meeting with Lady Kikyō (when he emerges from her toilet and prostrates himself before her) to the moment in *The Thousand Cherry Trees* when the fox Genkurō pops up through a trap door and bows before Lady Shizuka. More important, however, is the influence of *The Thousand Cherry Trees* on the seminal scene of the novel, where the pubescent hero Hōshimaru watches young women in an attic room where they dress the decapitated heads of dead enemy warriors, including a woman-head. The decisive inspiration here was less the amorous relationship between Shizuka and the fox, which is crucial to *Arrowroot,* than the relationship between Wakaba no Naishi and Kokingo.[22] Tanizaki recalled:

> The woman-head episode in Book II of *The Secret History of the Lord of Musashi* was clearly associated in my mind with the contrast between Kokingo's severed head and Wakaba no Naishi's beauty in Acts IV and V of *The Thousand Cherry Trees.* On the surface, there may appear to be no relationship between the heads and the women who entranced Hōshimaru . . . , on the one hand, and Kokingo and Wakaba no Naishi on the other; but there is a definite connection. In the play, as well, Wakaba no Naishi's beauty is emphasized by the presence of Kokingo's severed head. (And I, too, as a child–like Hōshimaru in *The Secret History*–felt the temptation to become a severed head and devote myself faithfully to Naishi.)
>
> (19:456–457)

Another likely source is *Oan monogatari,* an early-seventeenth-century chronicle that describes the 1600 siege of Ōgaki Castle, written by a daughter of one of the defending warriors. Her account includes this passage: "I remember that the heads taken by our side were brought together in the keep of the castle and a label was attached to each. . . . There is nothing frightening about a severed head. I slept among the heads. They smelled of blood."[23] Ibuki Kazuko recalls that Tanizaki asked her to buy a copy of *Oan monogatari* for him in 1960, when he was planning the sequel to *The Secret History.*[24]

Beyond its affinities with theater and with military chronicles, *The Secret History* also contains echoes of the Heian court. Lady Kikyō, in contrast to the unlettered samurai around her, comes from a noble Kyoto family. Her maternal grandfather has the courtly title "Middle Counselor of the Chrysanthemum Pavilion," and even her father, the commander of the Yakushiji army, is "more accomplished in poetry than in warfare" (41). Lady Kikyō is "naturally . . . proficient in Japanese poetry and other courtly accomplishments, since her mother was the daughter of a courtier and she herself had been reared in the capital" (94). It is not surprising, then, that she suggests an old-fashioned court entertainment–a poetry party– to cheer up her husband, or that one of her poems on the occasion alludes to the greatest of the court masterpieces, *The Tale of Genji.* In addition to providing an opportunity to make a cruel pun at Norishige's expense, the scene reinforces the contrast between Lady Kikyō, who alludes knowledgeably to the *Genji,* and Terukatsu, who has not read it and who realizes for the first time "that poetry was not to be slighted" (104).

Some of the relationships in *The Secret History* parallel relationships in the *Genji.* Shōsetsuin, innocent, childish, and generally disappointing to her husband, reminds one of Genji's last wife, the Third Princess. Neither marriage is successful, partly because the reluctant husband in each case is preoccupied with another woman—Genji with longing for Murasaki, Terukatsu "with thoughts of the inner palace at Mount Ojika" where Lady Kikyō lives (108). Lady Kikyō can be associated with Murasaki, then, but she recalls Genji's stepmother Fujitsubo even more. (Murasaki and Fujitsubo, niece and aunt, resemble each other so closely that Genji cherishes the latter as a substitute for the former; and so it is natural that Lady Kikyō should recall both.) Readers of the *Genji* will remember that after the old emperor has abdicated, his consort Fujitsubo spends more time with him than before: "She was always at his side, almost as if she were a common housewife."[25] Genji is distressed by her growing aloofness and finds it more difficult than ever to visit her. Terukatsu finds himself in the same situation when Lady Kikyō, "feeling real pity and sympathy for her husband's ugliness, . . . strove as a faithful wife and loving mother to redeem her former indiscretions" (141).[26]

These echoes of the Heian court and of the *Genji* cloak Lady Kikyō in an appropriately alluring aura that sets her apart from the crude warriors surrounding her, including Terukatsu. He idolizes her precisely because she *is* a superior being, in whose lovely hands he imagines himself being manipulated as a "ghastly head with an agonized expression" (30). The contrast between the Lady and himself is essential—she is the ideal beauty, while he (he prefers to think) is repulsive. In the castle attic he has identified most strongly with the ugliest of the heads (31) because they present the sharpest contrast with the girl Oteru, whose face "glowed with the pride and joy of the living, the embodiment of flawless beauty" (33). The uglier he is in his fantasies, the more beautiful the courtly Lady becomes.[27]

The novel carries the contrast between courtier and warrior so far that it occasionally lapses into a parody of the samurai code of honor.[28]

The Lord of Musashi, for example, though an "admirable child" (17) and "an unbending, stout hearted boy" (31), is motivated throughout his career not by honorable ambitions, as samurai-class hagiographers would have it, but by a bizarre masochistic fantasy that even he recognizes is "unbefitting the son of a samurai" (27). The samurai preoccupation with honor and dignity is satirized when Terukatsu meets Lady Kikyō for the first time:

> Lady Kikyō was used to having people leap from her toilet. . . .
> The shaft, which had often been used for this purpose, was provided with suitable footholds, so that a person might climb unsoiled and with the least possible strain into the room; and so Terukatsu was able to rise smartly through the black-lacquered rim and prostrate himself before her without resorting to postures that might impair his honor, and without compromising the lady's dignity.
> (75, 76)[29]

The parody is most savage in the description of the selfless devotion and death of Matoba Daisuke:

> [D]uring the four months that elapsed between splitting Norishige's lip and divesting him of an ear, Daisuke lay doubled up inside a cave-like cavity that had been specially dug near the top of the shaft [under lady Kikyō's toilet]. . . . From ancient times there have been numerous examples of men who sacrificed themselves for the sake of their masters, their parents, or their brothers; but there cannot have been many who endured the hardships suffered by Daisuke, secluded for four months beneath a toilet. The reader must not confuse Daisuke's behavior with the shameful conduct of a pervert or sex maniac. He was motivated by uncomplicated loyalty and filial piety. And probably, when this faithful, courageous youth realized that he had fulfilled his mission as far as he was able, he fell nobly on his sword, cast his body into the . . . darkness . . . , and literally sank into his grave.
> (89–90)[30]

As these passages belittle the samurai in relation to the court aristocracy, *The Secret History* also implicitly criticizes the historical literature produced by the samurai class. The novel contrasts itself again and again with "official" histories and emphasizes that the full story is not to be found in the standard sources. Tanizaki asserted that the Confucian orthodoxy embraced by the samurai class, especially during the Tokugawa period, had a deplorable effect on Japanese letters:

> We will never know how many geniuses were lost to so-called light literature thanks to the notion, current during the feudal period, that novels and the theater were for the diversion of women and children and were not suitable entertainment for samurai. A man of letters like Rai Sanyō [1780–1832], for example, had he not been confined by this thinking, would probably have written political or historical novels with some human warmth rather than that overly stiff *Unofficial History of Japan* [*Nihon gaishi*].
>
> (22:290)

The idea that fiction can tell us more about ourselves than history can is at least as old as *The Tale of Genji.* "*The Chronicles of Japan* and the rest are a mere fragment of the whole truth," Genji says to Tamakazura, in an often-quoted passage. "It is your romances that fill in the details."[31]

In the final analysis, though, *The Secret History* is not an attempt to set the record straight on sixteenth-century Japan. It aspires not to "fill in the details" omitted by the official histories, but to replace them with a vision based on the imagination—a vision that is truer to human experience than are the bare facts of history, especially when these are constrained by Confucian guidelines. Near the end of his life Tanizaki explained the genesis of his "historical" fiction: "However interesting the material may be, I have no desire to write about it, nor can I write about it, if it is not a fantasy born of my own mind. I have written one or two things that resemble historical fiction, but for the most part they are fabrications that I concocted: *A Blind Man's Tale, The Secret History of the Lord of Musashi, Kikigakishō* [1935], and *Captain Shigemoto's Mother* are all of this kind" (19:418). The works Tanizaki mentions here, and *Arrowroot* as well, assert the validity—indeed, the indispensability—of dreams and fantasies in our view of life. If we are satisfied passively to accept the accounts in the standard histories, human experience will mean little to us; but if we give rein to our fantasies, life past and present will breathe and throb inside us, and we will glimpse the truly seminal events taking place in those dark, secret places that only the imagination can probe.

FOUR

The Reed Cutter

An indication of the early reception of *The Reed Cutter,* published late in 1932, is the reluctance of Satō Haruo and Kubota Mantarō to read *A Portrait of Shunkin,* published in 1933, for fear that anything after *The Reed Cutter* would be a disappointment.[1] Another indication of the novella's success is that English translations of it and *Shunkin*—the first important English translations of Tanizaki—were published in 1936.[2]

As in *Arrowroot,* the opening pages of *The Reed Cutter* establish a setting that draws the reader away from the everyday world and anticipates the central themes of the story—a timeless place suspended between three provinces, a sand bar in the Yodo River near the intersection of Yamashiro, Kawachi, and Settsu, in a region where "even today the thatched houses lining the road on both sides look terribly antiquated to an eye that is accustomed to the Westernized towns and villages along the Hankyū Line" (7).[3] The primary narrator is a man of letters with antiquarian tastes, and, again as in *Arrowroot,* the focus of the work shifts gradually from him to a second narrator, and from the distant past of the primary narrator's researches to the more recent past of the second narrator's account. Similarly, the primary narrator begins with a factual, analytical view of things: though his presentation is lyrical, he is nonetheless attuned to strategy and geopolitics, but wine and atmosphere make him receptive to the dreamy romance of the story he hears. As in *Arrowroot,* the primary narrator is from Tokyo, his companion from Osaka. The stories told by the secondary narrators of *Arrowroot* and *The Reed*

Cutter are possible only in landscapes that are already steeped with phantoms of the past who serve as spurs to the imagination.

The "Ashikari" tradition goes back to at least the tenth century. Different versions appear in the tenth-century *Yamato monogatari* (Tales of Yamato; episode 148), the twelfth-century *Konjaku monogatarishū* (Tales of Times Now Past; book 30, number 5), the nō play *Ashikari,* and other works.[4] The poem that adorns the beginning of the novella appears in all of these and in an eleventh-century anthology:

Kimi nakute ashikarikeri to omou ni mo
itodo Naniwa no ura wa sumiuki[5]

How wretched I am without you, cutting reeds!
Life at Naniwa Bay grows harder still to bear.

(*Shūiwakashū,* no. 540)

The earliest and best-known is the *Yamato* version. A man and wife from Naniwa (the delta lands now occupied by the city of Osaka) are forced by poverty to separate. The wife marries a wealthy gentleman in Kyoto but cannot forget her first husband. She travels to Naniwa and discovers that he has been reduced to cutting reeds for a living. He hides in embarrassment when she inquires after him. When she sends her servant to him, he composes the "Ashikari" poem, and in reply she sends him her robe. The nō version is similar, except that the man and woman are happily reunited at Naniwa and return together to Kyoto. The central theme in the various versions of the "Ashikari" story is a reversal of the more common situation, in which the wife, left alone at home, longs for her husband, who has been away in the capital for a long time.[6]

There are obvious parallels between the ancient story and Tanizaki's adaptation. After the reluctant separation of Seribashi and Oyū, Oyū prospers as the wife of a wealthy Kyoto man, while Seribashi, left behind in Osaka, goes into decline. Presumably he could meet Oyū when he goes to her villa on the night of the full moon, but he chooses instead to gaze at her from a distance and to fondle the crepe under-robe she has left behind. The relationship between Seribashi and Oyū after their separation is something of a compromise between the unhappy ending of the *Yamato* version, where the man avoids his wife, and the joyful reunion of the nō version. A crucial reversal in Tanizaki's *Ashikari* is that the *man* goes looking for the *woman* (or, more precisely, looking *at* her).

Another conspicuous difference is the existence of the man in the reeds—Seribashi's son, who tells the story of his father and Oyū. He has no precedent in earlier versions of the story, and consequently his prominence in Tanizaki's novella is particularly noteworthy. His central position as the narrator's (and the reader's) only source of information on Seribashi and Oyū and as a participant in their story is carefully established.

The man professes to be the son of Seribashi and Oshizu, but as he himself says, "it's not that simple" (36). If he is Oshizu's son, why is he obsessed with his aunt, Oyū? The question has led Hata Kōhei to the conclusion that the man is the son of Oyū, not of Oshizu.[7] Reduced to the barest outline, Hata's thesis is that the man in the reeds is the son of Seribashi and Oyū, conceived during the half day when Oyū slips away from her son's sickbed, and born when Oyū is living with her family before her remarriage. Hata cites a number of passages as internal evidence in support of his argument, the most important of which are summarized in the following paragraphs. His analysis is revealing, whether or not one accepts his conclusions.

First, the theme of motherly love is established by the narrator's description of the landscape around Minase: "A scene like this one welcomes the traveler with a friendly smile, instead of startling the eye and enthralling the spirit. At a glance it would seem to be nothing, but standing here for a long time one is moved by a gentle affection, like the warm embrace of a loving mother" (11).

Second, when Seribashi tells his son about Oyū and shows him Oyū's robe, he sounds like a father telling a son about his mother, and he reminds one of such fathers and sons in *Captain Shigemoto's Mother* and *The Bridge of Dreams.*

Third, it is clear that Oshizu does her best to bring Oyū and Seribashi together, both emotionally and physically. On their wedding night Oshizu tells Seribashi, "I've come as your bride because I know my sister's heart. I couldn't face her if I gave myself to you. Make her happy, I beg you—I don't mind being your wife in name only" (36). When the three of them are together, Oshizu uses various tricks to urge Oyū and Seribashi toward greater intimacy:

> Oshizu may have been acting out of kindness—perhaps she thought that behaving this way would break down the reserve between Father and Miss Oyū, and that the momentum of events would lead them presently to open their hearts to each other. She seemed to be praying that momentum would build, that the two of them would commit some awkward blunder.
>
> (44)

Suggestions that Oshizu's efforts are successful come soon after she confesses to Oyū that she and Seribashi have never consummated their marriage. At first Oyū grows even more reserved than before, but "[p]resently the two sides drew together again, and Oshizu's plan went smoothly in the end" (45). Again: "Of course it was because of Oshizu's efforts on their behalf that *their relationship could develop this way*" (47, emphasis added). The crucial phrase is vague—*futari no aidagara ga sō iu fū ni narimashita*—and there is no clear antecedent for *sō iu fū* (this way). Hata is convincing when he argues that a physical relationship, promoted by Oshizu, is implied by these passages.

Fourth, the principal characters' denials are less than convincing. When the man in the reeds first says that Oshizu is his mother, he quickly adds, "but it's not that simple." Further, his denial that Seribashi and Oyū had physical relations is so hedged that it suggests the opposite:

> But here I must say something in defense of both Miss Oyū and Father—though their relationship had advanced this far, neither of them allowed it to go all the way. Oh, I suppose one could say that by now it made little difference whether they did or not, and it's no defense just to say that they didn't; but I want to believe Father.
>
> (47)

Seribashi's protestations of innocence to Oshizu are also suspect:

> After all that has happened, it's not a question of doing wrong by you, but I swear by the gods and Buddhas that we are faithful to you

> even when we sleep side by side. This may not be what you want, but Lady Oyū and I both would fear for our souls if we humiliated you that much. And so, well, we refrain for our own peace of mind. (47–48)

If Seribashi and Oyū have not yet had physical relations, there is nothing from this point on to prevent them. Oshizu has already demonstrated her eagerness to bring the two together and could easily overcome their scruples if she pressed a little more. In a significant juxtaposition, the memorable scene of Seribashi and his son adoring Oyū's under-robe immediately follows these dubious protestations of innocence.

Though the narrator has already been told that the man in the reeds is the son of Seribashi and Oshizu, the under-robe renews his suspicions. "If the relationship between Miss Oyū and your father was as you say," he asks, "then whose child are you?" The man confirms that this is the crucial question when he replies, "You may well ask. I can't bring my story to a close without telling you that" (49). He implies, then, that he has not yet answered the question, though he has already identified Oshizu as his mother.

He refers to Oshizu as his mother again, but only after narrating the death of Oyū's son Hajime, Oyū's return to her family, and her subsequent remarriage. These details are necessary to the man's answer because, according to Hata, they provide the true story and the exact chronology of the man's conception and birth. Seribashi's relationship with Oyū lasts, we are told, for "three or four years, beginning when Miss Oyū was twenty-three or -four," (49)[8] that is, until she is at least twenty-six, and possibly until she is twenty-eight. Her son Hajime dies when she is in her twenty-seventh year, and more than a year passes before she remarries. There is ample time for her to bear a child.

Hata finds several hints that she does bear a child. The "unflattering rumors" (50) can be taken as an indirect reference to Oyū's relationship with Seribashi and specifically to a pregnancy. It is decided that she should return to her own family "before things get complicated," (50) that is, before the child is born. Hata is specific about the timing: the child is conceived, he insists, during the half day that Oyū slips away from Hajime's sick bed.

According to Hata, then, the man in the reeds is conceived by Oyū when she is in her twenty-seventh year. He is close to fifty as he tells his story to the narrator; the narrator guesses as much even before the man says that his first visit to the Ogura villa, when he was "six or seven," (24) was "forty years ago" (26). Oyū, then, must be in her seventy-third to her seventy-sixth year, less than the "nearly eighty" assumed by the narrator.[9] If she is almost eighty, then the man in the reeds must have been born when she was about thirty, after her remarriage and after Seribashi has finally consummated his marriage with Oshizu. Hata believes that this tends to support his argument. The man himself never says that Oyū is almost eighty; the narrator, reverting to his characteristic rationality, makes this calculation based on his assumption that the man is Oshizu's son, conceived and born after Oyū's remarriage. Rather than answer the narrator's question and confirm that Oyū is his biological mother, the man disappears, leaving the narrator and the reader to guess the truth.

Finally, Hata discusses the ending in the light of Tanizaki's comments on the composition of *The Reed Cutter.* Up to the man's appearance in the reeds, Tanizaki recalled, he wrote with no clear conception of how the story would develop. As his thoughts took shape, he wrote to the end of the man's narrative but then could not think how to bring the story of the narrator, the man in the reeds, and Oyū to a conclusion. The man's disappearance was a last-minute inspiration (19:422). Hata suggests that Tanizaki's problem at the end actually was how to clinch the fact that the man is Oyū's son without being too obvious. Tanizaki's solution is to have the narrator guess Oyū's age on the assumption that the man is Oshizu's son, and to have the man disappear rather than clear up the misunderstanding definitively.[10]

Another element in *The Reed Cutter* tends to support the thesis that Seribashi and Oyū have a sexual relationship. As we have seen, Tanizaki's version incorporates the major elements of an ancient story, even to such details as location (Kyoto and Naniwa) and the lady's robe, left behind as a memento. These details, the title of the novella, and the opening poem direct attention to the old tale and invite the reader to draw parallels between it and the present work. The similarities between Tanizaki's novella and the early versions make comparison inevitable, while the differences between them attract attention to themselves and therefore take on special significance. The technique is akin to that of *honkadori*, or "allusive variation," practiced by certain court poets. Brower and Miner define *honkadori* as "echoing of words, sometimes only the situation or conception, of a well-known earlier poem in such a way that recognizable elements are incorporated into a new meaning, but one in which the meaning of the earlier poem also enters, in a manner distinguished from mere borrowing and use of similar materials and expressions."[11] When a poet employs the *honkadori* technique, the new poem is meaningful on one level even to a reader unfamiliar with the tradition; but for the reader who recognizes and considers the echo, the new poem has greater richness and depth. In the case of *The Reed Cutter*, the echo is that of the early tradition, most familiar from *Yamato monogatari* and the nō play *Ashikari*. Tanizaki uses a similar technique in *The Bridge of Dreams*, in which the reader's understanding is enhanced by a knowledge of *The Tale of Genji*.

In *Yamato monogatari* and the nō *Ashikari* the man and the woman are married, but their equivalents in Tanizaki's work—Seribashi and Oyū—are not. This sort of discrepancy between the tradition and the new version demands an explanation. The simplest conclusion is that Seribashi and Oyū are husband and wife in all but name. In other words, the text calls upon the reader to apply knowledge of the tradition to the present work, to fill the gaps in the information supplied by the narrator. To an unquestioning reader, unfamiliar with the tradition, *The Reed Cutter* may be obscure and perplexing; but to the alert reader the hints that Hata identifies offer a challenge.

Hata has not "proven" that Oyū is the mother of the man in the reeds; after all, the man is unambiguous when he finally says "I was borne by Oshizu" (52). Hata's "evidence" is not conclusive. The same can be said of the *honkadori* analysis. *The Reed Cutter* was read with pleasure for more than forty years and hailed as a masterpiece before anyone suggested in print that Oyū might be the man's mother, and even now Hata's thesis has not been accepted by everyone.[12] Ambiguity is part of the novella's charm. Ultimately, Hata's unequivocal reading has the same effect as the kabuki spotlights that *In Praise of Shadows* deplores.

The man in the reeds has good reason to be drawn to Oyū, whether she is his biological mother or not. Oshizu dies when he is about five years old, leaving an emotional vacuum that he fills with images of the Ideal Mother, personified by the woman his father venerates—Oyū. In short, he is pursuing a vision of Mother, as the lonely sons in *Haha o Kouru Ki* (Longing for Mother, 1919), *Arrowroot, Captain Shigemoto's Mother,* and *The Bridge of Dreams* are doing. Having inherited his father's outlook, he identifies the Ideal Mother with his father's Ideal Lover.

The clearest manifestation of the man's inheritance is his annual repetition of Seribashi's ritual visit to Oyū's villa. The man goes to peer at Oyū through the hedge not only as a child yearning for his mother, but also as the heir to his father's romantic love for her. The man in the reeds describes the father-to-son transference twice. Early in his account, he recalls what his father said the first time he told his son about Oyū:

> This isn't the sort of thing a child will understand, he'd say, but soon you, too, will be an adult. Remember what I've told you and try to call it to mind when you get older. I'll speak to you as if an adult were listening, and not a child. Father's face was grave whenever he said this, and he spoke as though he were with a friend his own age. (28)

The process by which love is passed from father to son is demonstrated concretely when Seribashi shows Oyū's under-robe to his son:

> Miss Oyū wore this against her skin. See how heavy the crepe is. I took it in my hands. It was quite unlike the modern fabric—the crepe of those days was deeply crimped and the threads were thick, so that it seemed as heavy as chain mail. Heavy, don't you think? he asked. It truly is, I said. He nodded as though my answer gratified him. Crepe doesn't have to be limp and soft, he said; the real value of the material is in this heavy crimping. You can feel the softness of a woman's skin all the better if you touch her body through these heavy crimps. Crepe looks rougher and more beautiful and feels better to the touch, the smoother the skin of the person wearing it. Miss Oyū was born with delicate hands and feet, and their delicacy showed all the more clearly when she wore this heavy crepe. He held up the robe with both hands. I don't know how her body supported this much weight, he said with a sigh. He rubbed his cheek against it as though he were embracing her.
>
> Then you must have been quite grown up by the time your father showed you the underrobe, I said, having listened to the man's story

> in silence up to this point. I should think it would be difficult for a young boy to understand something like that. No, I was still only about ten, but Father spoke as though I were an adult. I didn't understand at the time, of course, but I remembered his words and gradually worked out their meaning as I matured.
>
> (48–49)

Oyū is one of the most striking embodiments of the ideal lover and mother for whom Tanizaki's men and boys long. She seems to be the first of Tanizaki's heroines consciously modelled after Nezu (née Morita) Matsuko, who was to become Tanizaki's third wife a few years later and remain with him until his death. On November 8, 1932, he wrote to her, "I am now working on the continuation of *The Reed Cutter,* which began in last month's issue of *Kaizō.* The plot has nothing to do with you; but I hope you will not be offended to know that I am thinking of you as I describe the heroine's character. . . . I have asked Mr. Higuchi [Tomimaro] to do the illustrations. I would like him to model the heroine's face after yours, but I am too embarrassed to tell him so directly" (24:300–301). In the same letter he writes, "Someday when the opportunity arises I want to announce to the world that all my works from a certain time were written under your influence." More than thirty years later, he did as he had promised: *The Reed Cutter* is, he revealed, "the first thing I wrote with Matsuko clearly in mind" (19:398).

At the same time, it would be misleading to say that Oyū is modelled after Matsuko. Sachiko, in *The Makioka Sisters,* is an idealized but nonetheless recognizable portrait of Matsuko. Oyū, on the other hand, is an embodiment of Tanizaki's fantasies about Matsuko, or about the Ideal Woman as represented by Matsuko. The same can be said of other Tanizaki heroines apparently inspired by her: Lady Oichi in *A Blind Man's Tale,* Lady Kikyō in *The Secret History of the Lord of Musashi,* Shunkin, and Shigemoto's mother. In all these works the author is like a painter who cannot work without a living model, but whose paintings do not necessarily resemble the model.

Oyū is portrayed as an ingenuous, childlike woman who takes for granted luxury and the devotion of those around her. It never occurs to her that life could be different, and her friends and relatives, for their part, consider it natural to wait on her:

> Being "a person of character," to borrow my aunt's words, Miss Oyū didn't ask people to treat her this way, nor was she arrogant or pushy, but everyone was extremely kind to her, waiting on her as if she were a princess and allowing her to do as she pleased, determined not to let her suffer the slightest anxiety. They sought to keep her untouched by the everyday troubles of the world, even if it meant sacrificing themselves for her sake. It was Miss Oyū's nature to make everyone who came near her feel this way, including her parents, sisters, and friends. When my aunt visited Miss Oyū as a girl, Miss Oyū was treated as though she were the Kosobe family treasure. She never did the smallest chore herself, and her sisters looked after her like chambermaids; nor was there anything unnatural about this, my aunt said—Miss Oyū seemed to accept the attention with the greatest innocence.
>
> (32)

Oyū's waywardness is playful and innocent, her pranks harmless:

> Once she held her hand in front of Father's nose and said, I want you to hold your breath until I say all right. Father made a great effort but finally let a little breath escape. I haven't said all right yet, Miss Oyū cried peevishly. So she'd close his lips with her fingers or use a folded piece of red Shioze crepe to cover his mouth. At times like this, Father said, her face would look like the face of a kindergarten child, and one could hardly believe that she was a woman over twenty.
>
> (46)

She also has a theatrical streak. Seribashi tells his son,

> Miss Oyū was born with a sense of theater; her thoughts and gestures were spontaneously theatrical, which enhanced her cheerful personality and added to her charm without ever seeming artificial or affected; and the greatest difference between Oshizu and Miss Oyū was that Oshizu lacked this sense of theater. No one but Miss Oyū could have been in her element playing the koto in a long formal robe, or sitting behind a curtain of robes and drinking saké from a lacquered cup as a chambermaid poured for her.
>
> (46–47)[13]

Thus Oyū takes a child's pleasure in playing the part of a court lady, wearing a flamboyant robe at her recital, and acting the role of mistress to Seribashi's steward when they travel together.

The reader never has a chance to "see" Oyū, nor does the narrator, since everything is filtered through the man and his father. The narrative technique thus serves to distance Oyū from the reader. Her appearance is never described clearly. When the boy and his father peer at her from the garden hedge, her face is hidden by a flower arrangement. Later, Seribashi describes her to his son in terms of haze and mist:

> There are other women with features as beautiful as hers, but there's something indistinct about her face. Her features—the eyes, the nose, the mouth—are blurred as though they were veiled by a layer of silk gauze, leaving no strong, clear lines; and when I gaze at her face a misty shadow seems to fall before my eyes, as if a haze floated about her and nowhere else.
>
> (30–31)

Since he sees her as an ideal, Seribashi does not recognize individual traits that would set her apart as a distinct person. Similar techniques of indirection and obfuscation can be found in other Tanizaki portraits of the Ideal Woman, as in *A Portrait of Shunkin, Captain Shigemoto's Mother,* and *The Bridge of Dreams.*

Another aspect of Oyū's characterization is her association with ladies of the Heian court. Even before Oyū is introduced, the man in the reeds is subtly likened to the Heian courtier who searches the bamboo forest of Sagano for the Emperor's beloved Kogō and, drawn by the sound of her koto, finally discovers her on the night of the full moon. The man in the reeds sings part of the nō *Kogō* under the full moon of the Eighth Month, then tells of being drawn to Oyū's villa as "[t]he sounds of koto, samisen, and kokyū drifted toward us from deep within the trees" (25).[14] The narrator strengthens the parallel by observing that the Minase landscape resembles that of Saga (10).

Oyū's villa at Lake Ogura, with its moon-viewing banquets and spacious garden, also resembles a Heian mansion—in particular, ex-Emperor Gotoba's Minase Palace, lovingly evoked by the narrator; and the man's first glimpse of Oyū in her villa is in the tradition of the Heian romances. Like countless Heian gentlemen (and like Tsumura, in *Arrowroot*), the man in the reeds finds the lady of his dreams in a rural setting and gazes at her through a hedge. The scene is especially reminiscent of Kaoru's first view of the Uji sisters as they amuse themselves with music at an estate just upstream from Lake Ogura; and when she urges Seribashi to marry her sister, Oyū recalls the older Uji sister pleading with Kaoru to take her younger sister.

Oyū lives in the style of a court lady even before moving to her villa, scenting her robes with incense and leaning on an armrest, surrounded by the trappings of courtly luxury. In this regard she meets Seribashi's requirements perfectly. "Father's tastes might be described as lordly or courtly. That is, he didn't want a chic woman but someone refined, like a lady of the court, one worthy to be dressed in a long formal robe, seated behind a curtain stand, and given the *Genji* to read" (30).[15] She wears an *uchikake* and burns incense when she plays *Yuya* at her recital. "The koto was of no importance," she declares afterward, "but I did want a chance to dress like this just once. Reluctant to take off the robe, she added, "And now I'm going to have my picture taken" (33). Finally, in her photograph "she has a quality about her that recalls the subtle ladies of the court, a classical aroma in the midst of radiant good cheer, such as one senses in the face of an old Izukura doll" (31).

Oyū's characterization is enhanced by the contrasting portrayal of her sister Oshizu. The difference between the two is suggested by their names. *Yū* (also read *asobi*) signifies pleasure, play, or travel; in *The Reed Cutter* it appears in such compounds as *on-asobi* (concert) and *asobiwaza* (entertainments, 13:444); *yūen* (banquet, 13:446); *gyoyū* ([royal] entertainments, 13:450); *yūjo* (courtesan, 13:453); and *yūgei* (polite accomplishments, 13:456). *Shizu*, on the other hand, connotes quiet. Oyū is vivacious and childlike, Oshizu quiet; Oyū is willful, Oshizu selfless; Oyū is spontaneous, Oshizu calculating; Oyū takes for granted the devotion of others, and Oshizu is unquestioningly devoted to her. A similar pair can be found in *The Makioka Sisters*—Sachiko is so much livelier than her younger sister Yukiko that she is asked to stay at home when Yukiko goes to meet a potential husband. (The similarity is not coincidental—both pairs were inspired by Matsuko and her sister Shigeko.) Oshizu is attractive but lacks her sister's theatricality and her special kind of beauty, expressed by the archaic word *rōtaketa*. *Rōtashi*, the original form, has been translated as "pretty" or "winsome" or "petitely charming" or "demure" by Edward Seidensticker, who observes that "with related and variant forms it appears in *The Tale of Genji* close to two hundred times, in thirty-four of the fifty-four chapters."[16] By virtue of its extensive use in the *Genji* and other Heian literature, *rōtashi* takes on additional connotations of classical elegance when used by a modern writer. It is precisely this quality of timeless charm that Oyū possesses and Oshizu lacks.

In a broader sense, a courtly tone for the novella is established at the outset by the "Ashikari" poem and sustained by Tanizaki's prose. Reminiscent of the prose of the Heian romances, the text of *The Reed Cutter* is characterized by long sentences, few Chinese characters, and little punctuation. Quotation marks are almost totally lacking—dialogue is set off from narrative by verb forms and context. All these features are characteristics of Heian texts but unusual in modern Japanese.

Inspired by memories of the classics, the narrator lets his imagination stray back to the age of Gotoba and falls into a reverie: "While I was lost in these reflections, my daydreams wandered here and there, sketching visions of those times, and deep in my ears I could hear the lingering tones of the strings and winds, the murmur of the waters on the lake, and finally even the happy voices of the nobles and courtiers" (13). Just as Gotoba himself, in a passage quoted from *Masukagami*, strives to recapture the subtle elegance of the world of the *Genji*, the narrator's evocation of court life helps to establish an atmosphere appropriate for Oyū.

But the court is not the only aspect of Heian society that the narrator recalls. When he goes back to the river after dinner, his meditations turn to the ladies of pleasure who frequented the river banks in ancient times. "Would it be impossible to raise them to the surface of this stream for a time," he muses, "like bubbles forming on the water—these women who likened themselves to avatars of Samantabhadra and were even revered by a venerable sage?" (18) When the man appears in the reeds, the narrator asks about the women: "Do you suppose that courtesans like the Lady of Eguchi poled their boats around this sandbar? That, more than anything else, is what I see as I look at the moon—visions of those women floating dimly before my eyes" (22). His companion has similar thoughts and "[is] sketching visions of the past" (23) as he views the moon, but he tells the narrator not about the ancient courtesans (*yūjo*), but about Oyū. Thus Oyū is unmistakably associated with the women who plied their trade on the Yodo River, and in particular with the Lady of Eguchi, as well as with the ladies of the court.[17]

The narrator's mention of the Lady of Eguchi and of the poet-priest Saigyō (1118–1190) alludes to a famous anecdote that is of central significance. A discussion of this anecdote will lead to the complex subject of the relationship between *The Reed Cutter* and the nō.

On a pilgrimage to the Shitennōji monastery in Naniwa, Saigyō is caught in a cloudburst. At Eguchi he asks a woman for lodging. When she turns him away, he addresses this poem to her:

> Yo no naka o itou made koso katakarame
> kari no yadori o oshimu kimi kana
>
> The world of love must indeed be hard to put aside—
> But selfishly you deny me even this fleeting shelter!

The woman replies:

> Yo o itou hito to shi kikeba
> kari no ya ni kokoro tomu na to omou bakari zo
>
> Hearing that you are one who shuns the world of love
> I worry lest you dwell upon this fleeting, borrowed shelter.[18]

The nō play *Eguchi* combines this episode with a tradition that certain courtesans were avatars of the bodhisattva Samantabhadra (Fugen Bosatsu). Tanizaki summarizes one version of the legend in *A Tale of Chrysanthemums in Chaos*, which he wrote two years before *The Reed Cutter:*

> According to Saigyō's *Senjūshō* and local tradition, it was believed that Hanaurushi was in reality an avatar of Samantabhadra. . . . It is said that Shōkū Shōnin, the founder of the Shoshasan monastery in the Province of Harima, prayed that he might see the avatar of a bodhisattva. One night in a dream he was told, "To the southwest is a port called Muro. The mistress there, a *shirabyōshi* dancer called Hanaurushi, is an avatar of Samantabhadra."

Finding Hanaurushi, Shōkū watches her dance, but each time he closes his eyes he sees Samantabhadra on a white elephant, his traditional mount. Weeping with joy, Shōkū begins to worship Hanaurushi, whereupon she mounts a white elephant and flies away into the western sky.[19] The narrator of *The Reed Cutter* is referring to this tradition when he says that courtesans "were even revered by a venerable sage."

The result of this synthesis in the nō *Eguchi* is that the Lady of Eguchi, with whom Saigyō exchanges poems, turns into Samantabhadra at the end of the play and "rides off to the western skies" on her pleasure boat, which has turned into a white elephant.[20] Even before she is revealed as Samantabhadra, the Lady of Eguchi is repeatedly associated with the bright, full moon of autumn, which is in turn a conventional symbol of Buddhist enlightenment. Thus the lady represents human desire on several levels: physical beauty, the beauty of the moon, and, ultimately, the elimination of desire through grasping the truth of Buddhism. When the narrator of *The Reed Cutter* sees visions of the Lady of Eguchi on a moonlit night, his visions must be not only of a courtesan, but also of the bodhisattva; and the "visions of the past" that the man is pursuing are of the same dual nature, sensual and spiritual. The difference is that the narrator is thinking of the Lady of Eguchi; his companion, of Oyū.[21]

It is not far-fetched to associate a courtesan with Samantabhadra and Oyū with a courtesan. The notion that the Lady of Eguchi is an avatar of Samantabhadra "illustrates the Mahayana doctrine that even the meanest creature in the world is potentially a Bodhisattva."[22] In fact, a courtesan is particularly appropriate for this role, because "like beauty and enlightenment themselves, she is available to all."[23] At the heart of it is a sense that sexual ecstasy and religious ecstasy are related, and that the one can lead to the other—a sense that the veneration of beauty is close to being a religious experience.[24] It is so for the man in the reeds and his father.

Oyū is not "the meanest creature," nor is she "available to all," but she does share beauty, the power to inspire religious feelings in the men who love her, and one other quality with the Eguchi courtesan. It is helpful to consider what *Chrysanthemums in Chaos* says about the courtesan who turns out to be Samantabhadra:

> The reader must not confuse ancient courtesans with those of more recent times. The first Murogimi, Hanaurushi, was truly the "kimi" ["mistress"] of Muro, as her title suggests—she was the local "country-baron's daughter"—and only those of the highest rank, court nobles

> and generals and the like, could hope to be received as her guests. Consider the fact that the remains of five monasteries built by the first Murogimi can be seen even today. With that kind of wealth and power, Hanaurushi was surely the mistress of that beautiful seaport, both in name and in fact.
>
> (12:219–220)

Like Hanaurushi, Oyū is a *chōja no musume*, which I have translated as "country-baron's daughter." This is a stock type, typically the daughter of a rich man who lives in the country, pampered, sheltered, naive, spoiled, and willful. Suitors long for her from a distance but either give up because she is too far above them or, if they persist, find her difficult or impossible to win. The prototype in Japanese literature is Kaguya-hime, the Shining Princess in the tenth-century *Taketori monogatari* (Tale of the Bamboo Cutter). This pampered, willful stepdaughter of a rich bamboo cutter sets impossible tasks for her five noble suitors, and rejects them one by one. In the end she returns to her true home, the Palace of the Moon.[25] Tamakazura and the Uji sisters in the *Genji* are ladies in the same tradition, as is Yukiko in *The Makioka Sisters.* Oyū is not troubled by large numbers of suitors, but is a typical *chōja no musume* in every other respect.

There is, then, a clear line from Hanaurushi in the *Senjūshō* to the Lady of Eguchi in the nō and finally to Oyū. The pampered daughter of a wealthy family, Oyū lives the luxurious life of a Heian court lady and, at the same time, of a high-ranking Heian courtesan; and like Hanaurushi and the Lady of Eguchi, she is the object of both physical and spiritual longing. For the father and son, she is a bodhisattva, as the courtesans were believed to be.

These men are not alone among Tanizaki's characters in regarding the woman they love with religious reverence. To Jōji, Naomi's body is "more perfect . . . than the Buddhas of Nara," and he feels "a deep, religious sense of gratitude well up" as he gazes at her photographs. Near the end of the novel she has become "a precious object of yearning and adoration," before whom Jōji can "only kneel and offer worship."[26] For Kaname, in *Some Prefer Nettles,* "a woman had to be either a goddess or a plaything." For him to admire anything, "it had to have about it a certain radiance, the power to inspire veneration. One had to feel forced to one's knees before it, or lifted by it to the skies. . . . A woman-worshipper, he looked for the same divine attributes in women."[27] In *Manji* (Quicksand, 1928–1930), Mitsuko is the model for her lover's portrait of the bodhisattva Avalokiteśvara (in Japanese, Kannon). Other examples are discussed in Chapters Five and Seven.

Eguchi is representative of the form known as *mugen*, or "dream-phantom," nō. A traveling priest stops at Eguchi, where he hears about the Lady of Eguchi from a villager. When the priest recites Saigyō's poem, a village woman appears out of nowhere and engages him in conversation, reciting the poem that the Lady of Eguchi had composed in reply. The village woman turns out to be the ghost of the Lady of Eguchi. After a brief interlude, she reenters in her true form, riding in a pleasure boat. She sings and dances for the priest, then turns into Samantabhadra and rises into the western sky. The priest is the *waki*, or "sideman," whose function, as we have seen in *Arrowroot*, is to elicit the story from the *shite* (protagonist), in this case the ghost. Before the interlude, when she is a village woman, she is referred to as the *maejite* and afterwards, when she reappears in her true form, as the *nochijite*. In some *mugen* plays, such as *Hotoke no hara*, there is a suggestion that the *waki* is asleep and dreaming when the *nochijite* appears.

The structure of Tanizaki's *The Reed Cutter* is close to that of *Eguchi*. It is hard to know which play or plays served as a model for the novella, but *Eguchi* is a likely candidate, and in any case it is clear that Tanizaki borrowed and adapted the *mugen* nō structure. The narrator is the *waki*, the man in the reeds the *shite*. Though not a priest, the narrator is a traveler with a deep interest in the history and legends of the region he visits. Since he already knows about the Eguchi courtesans, he needs no villager to tell him about them. As in *Eguchi*, the *shite*—the man in the reeds—appears out of nowhere, drawn by the *waki*'s poetry recitation. The poem that stirs the man in the reeds to introduce himself is Po Chü-i's *Lute Song* (*Biwakō* or *P'i-p'a hsing*), about a former courtesan from the capital whom the poet has seen on a boat singing the story of her life and accompanying herself on the lute. The narrator and the man in the reeds talk and drink together. When the narrator asks about the Eguchi courtesans, the man begins the story of his father's relationship with Oyū. The narrator prods him and asks leading questions when the man pauses in his story. As the audience of a nō play perceives a warrior's agony or the anguish of a woman's love through the *waki*'s dream, the reader of *The Reed Cutter* sees Oyū and Seribashi faintly through the filter of the narrator's account. Tanizaki's *waki*, here and in *Arrowroot*, are more skeptical and persistent than most of their counterparts in the nō and are more individualized, but the correspondence to the *mugen* form is close none the less.

The *shite* in *Eguchi* states her position by summarizing the poem with which she has replied to Saigyō. The man in the reeds suggests his own frame of mind by singing two classical pieces, the nō *Kogō* and lines from a Chinese Buddhist poem. As we have seen, *Kogō* recounts a courtier's search for the emperor's favorite lady. The lines from the Chinese poem are, "The moon glows on the river, wind rustles in the pines; / what is the reason for this long, clear night?"[28] In Ueda Akinari's "Aozukin" ("The Blue Hood," one of the tales in *Ugetsu monogatari*), the same verse is assigned to a priest who has been driven mad by lust. "Without leaving this spot you must meditate quietly," he is told, "and when you have the meaning of the verse, you will of your own accord rediscover the true mind of a Buddha." The priest recites the verse over and over as he attempts to find release from his lust, and in the end melts away "as frost that meets the morning sun."[29] Most readers who recognize the verse would associate it with Akinari's chilling story.

These selections suggest two things about the man's state of mind as he sings them. The first associates him with the Heian courtier who ventures out on the night of the full moon in search of the beautiful Kogō and ultimately finds her by following the drifting tones of her koto. The second identifies him with a priest who struggles to overcome his obsessive desires and "rediscover the true mind of a Buddha." The man in the reeds is, in short, an obsessive searcher who longs for release; he is like the ghosts in the nō who cling lovingly, jealously, or angrily to those whom they love or hate and who seek release from their attachments by telling their stories to the *waki* and asking him to pray for them. Like Akinari's mad monk, the man in the reeds vanishes at the end of *The Reed Cutter*, but unlike the monk, he has not been released from his obsession—he is off to gaze longingly at Oyū again. On the other hand, if she is the bodhisattva of tradition, then his pursuit of her image might lead him to enlightenment.

The nō analogy raises new questions about the man's identity. In most *mugen* nō plays, the *shite* is a ghost and appears in two forms—first in the shape of a local person (*maejite*) and then in his or her true form (*nochijite*). This suggests that the man in the reeds may be his father's ghost, and that he has two identities, *mae* and *nochi.*[30] His appearance and disappearance are ghostly, to be sure, but it is unclear whether he is literally a ghost. What is clear is that psychologically the man in the reeds is both father and son. Physically he may be the son, but he has inherited his father's feelings toward Oyū. In a sense, then, the man *is* possessed by his father's ghost, but there is no clear demarcation between *mae-* and *nochijite*—no point at which one can say with confidence that the son has turned into the ghost of the father. The possession is in the form of a psychological inheritance; the man shares his father's frame of mind without ever ceasing to be himself. He is simultaneously ghost and non-ghost, *maejite* and *nochijite*, father and son.

We have seen that *The Reed Cutter* is thematically and structurally indebted to the nō, particularly to *Eguchi*, and that it alludes to the nō plays *Ashikari* and *Kogō.* Mention must be made of one more related play. The *Yuya* that Oyū plays at her recital is a composition by Yamada Kengyō (1757–1817), based on a nō play of the same name.[31] In both versions, the beautiful Yuya, favorite of Taira no Munemori, pleads with her master for permission to visit her dying mother. Munemori refuses at first because he wants Yuya's company at his own cherry-blossom party, but in the end he consents. In several ways this piece is appropriate to Oyū and to the novella. The play is about a child's love for her mother—a love that takes precedence over all other considerations of duty and loyalty—and so reference to it subtly reinforces the same theme in *The Reed Cutter.* The name Yuya is an alternate reading of the characters for Kumano, a place identified with Fudaraku (in Sanskrit, Potalaka), the home of the bodhisattva Avalokiteśvara; and Munemori's cherry-blossom party takes place at Kiyomizu Temple, where the principal object of worship is Avalokiteśvara. Yuya, then, is identified with Avalokiteśvara, just as Oyū is implicitly identified with

Samantabhadra. ("Yuya" is also the professional name of one of the courtesans mentioned by the narrator.) These parallels between *Yuya* and *The Reed Cutter* should not be pressed too far, but they illustrate the care with which Tanizaki chose his details. Upon close examination, an apparently casual mention of *Yuya* turns out to be related to the central themes of the novella.

From this ramble through *Ashikari*'s classical sources, we can now return to the focal point of the novella and conclude. *The Reed Cutter* is the story of a man's longing for a mother-lover figure—an idealized, unattainable woman to whom he is devoted with something like religious fervor, whom he perceives as a sort of bodhisattva. It is the story of a man who combines his father's physical and romantic longings with the longings of a child separated from his mother, and with a spiritual longing for the ideal.

FIVE

A Portrait of Shunkin

A Portrait of Shunkin, Tanizaki's most celebrated novella, was hailed as a modern classic as soon as it was published in June, 1933. Satō Haruo considered it the finest in the series of Tanizaki masterpieces that began with *Arrowroot,* and Masamune Hakuchō, noting that Tanizaki continued to write energetically even after *Shunkin* was published, urged him to take a rest, because "*monogatari* writers of the Heian period achieved immortal fame with only one or two works of the caliber of *A Blind Man's Tale* or *A Portrait of Shunkin.*"[1] *Shunkin* was also successful with the public. The first two hardback printings (which also contain *The Reed Cutter* and Tanizaki's last play, *Kaoyo*) are notable for their elegant black- and red-lacquer covers. They sold so fast that the lacquerers could not keep pace with orders and had to give up. An unlacquered edition published in the summer of 1934 went through sixty printings in its first year.[2] The popularity of *A Portrait of Shunkin* has continued to the present, the story having been adapted to the opera stage, to the Bunraku puppet theater, and, at least five times, to the screen.

Tanizaki's interest in Western literature is part of the context in which *Shunkin* was written. Two Western stories were formative influences. It was Satō Haruo who first suggested a connection between *Shunkin* and Thomas Hardy's tale "Barbara, of the House of Grebe," which Tanizaki had translated into Japanese in 1927. Tanizaki confirmed his friend's observation. The story of Shunkin and Sasuke developed, Tanizaki said, as he reversed the roles of the man and the woman and asked himself what a Japanese man in Barbara's position would have done.[3] A likely connection with a story by Arthur Schnitzler (1862–1931) was suggested to me when Tanizaki Matsuko mentioned Schnitzler as one of the authors (along with Balzac) whom her husband had admired, and recalled Tanizaki's urging her in the early 1930s to read Schnitzler's "The Blind Geronimo and His Brother."[4]

Both *Shunkin* and Schnitzler's story are about a blind musician (Shunkin, Geronimo) and a devoted attendant (Sasuke, Carlo). In Schnitzler's story, the elder brother, Carlo, has blinded the younger, Geronimo, in a childhood accident. When Geronimo is fifteen, he begins to support Carlo and himself as a beggar-minstrel, entertaining travellers at roadside inns by playing the guitar and singing. Carlo, motivated by love and remorse, is determined to devote his life to his brother. One day a mysterious traveller gives Carlo one franc for Geronimo's performance, but tells Geronimo that he has paid twenty francs and warns him not to let Carlo cheat him. Geronimo's latent distrust and resentment of Carlo come to the surface. Carlo is miserable.

> The blind man's suspicion was not a thing of today; it must have lain dormant in him, and only the occasion, or, perhaps the courage had lacked for him to express it openly. And all that Carlo had done for him had been in vain; vain was his penance, vain the sacrifice of his entire life. What was he to do now? Should he continue day after day, for who knows how much longer, to lead him through his eternal night, watch over him, beg for him, and have no other reward but distrust and curses?
>
> . . . He could not and did not want to desert him. He either had to bear his mistrust, or find some way to convince the blind man of the groundlessness of his suspicion.[5]

To persuade his brother that he is not holding back twenty francs, Carlo steals that amount from travellers staying at the inn; but when he gives the gold coin to Geronimo, the blind man only grows angrier: "But I know you are lying! You are lying all the time! You've lied a hundred times already! You wanted to keep this for yourself too, but you were afraid, that's all!"[6] Only when the brothers are arrested for the theft does Geronimo realize that Carlo has stolen for his sake.

Schnitzler was close to Freud and had a particular interest in psychiatry, and so it is not surprising that the emphasis in "The Blind Geronimo and His Brother" is on Carlo's feelings of guilt, his devotion to Geronimo, his need for Geronimo's love, and his longing to be "his own"; and on Geronimo's suspicious response, his reluctance to admit his need for Carlo, and his final recognition of their mutual dependence and love. The parallels with *A Portrait of Shunkin* are suggestive. In each story, despite the titles, the attendant is the central character and the narrative presents his point of view.[7] Carlo, like Sasuke, learns to empathize with his blind companion. At first he acts "as if his eyes were ashamed of the light which was granted to them, but of which they could not give a single ray to the blind brother"; and later, "it seemed as if he could see the night through which Geronimo walked by his side."[8] In each story, the intimate but incomplete relationship between the blind musician and the attendant is tested and emerges stronger and more complete, thanks to a sacrifice on the part of the attendant—Carlo steals a gold piece; Sasuke, who has become Shunkin's lover as well as her servant and pupil, blinds himself when she is disfigured by scalding burns. Both stories demonstrate that a blind person does not necessarily appreciate the attendant's pity and devotion; the blind can be proud, resentful, suspicious, and willful; and the attendant is happy only when he has proven his dedication and selflessness. Thus both Carlo and Sasuke debase themselves, and both Geronimo and Shunkin arrive at a new understanding of their love and of the reciprocity of their relationship. Finally, the scene in which Geronimo forgives Carlo both resembles and contrasts with the moment when Sasuke first tells Shunkin of his self-inflicted blindness:

> He saw Geronimo smile in a mild, perfectly happy fashion, such as he had not seen since his childhood days. And Carlo smiled too. It seemed as if nothing terrible could happen to him now—neither at court, nor anywhere else in the world. He had found his brother again . . . No, he was really his own for the first time.[9]

> All Shunkin replied was: "Really, Sasuke?" She sat there a long while, sunk in thought. Never before or since did Sasuke experience such happiness as during those moments of silence.[10]
>
> (74)

Both Carlo and Sasuke find peace, but it is not clear that Shunkin is as happy as Geronimo.

In Hardy's story, Barbara Grebe rejects the suit of the Earl of Uplandtowers and elopes with a beautiful young man named Willowes, whose "blood was, as far as they knew, of no distinction whatever."[11] Willowes is half blinded and hideously disfigured in a fire. Barbara's love is inadequate to the shock—she can no longer bear to look at her husband. Willowes decides to give her some time and goes away, but he dies before he can return. The memory of his beauty haunts Barbara even after she has finally married Uplandtowers. She secretly acquires a marble statue made in Willowes's likeness, which she visits and adores until Uplandtowers discovers it. He has the statue mutilated to match Willowes's appearance after the fire and places it in a closet before the bed. Night after night, as they lie together, Uplandtowers forces Barbara to look at the horrible likeness in an attempt to quash her love for Willowes and gain it for himself. He succeeds, but Barbara's spirit is broken and she soon dies.

Several earlier works bear the marks of Tanizaki's reading of Hardy. In the play *Eien no gūzō* (Eternal Image, 1922), a young sculptor carves an image of the woman he loves; in another play, *Homboku yawa* (An Evening Tale from Homboku, 1922), a man and wife disfigure each other with sulfuric acid.[12] *The Secret History of the Lord of Musashi* contains even more striking parallels with "Barbara." Lady Kikyō's husband, like Barbara's, is disfigured. Even the details of his mutilation (a harelip, no nose, and a missing ear) are similar to those spelled out by Hardy:

> [T]he school-master drew upon a paper a sketch of the disfigured head of Willowes, explaining, with bated breath, the various details in the representation.
>
> "It was very strange and terrible!" said Lord Uplandtowers, taking the sketch in his hand. "Neither nose nor ears!"[13]

The telling contrast is that Lady Kikyō's love for her husband grows stronger the more he is mutilated. She sacrifices her affair with Terukatsu and, at the end of the novel, is the devoted wife that Barbara could not be. "[F]or the first time a complete love developed between them, and Norishige lived with an emotional fulfillment such as he had never experienced before."[14] In *A Portrait of Shunkin*, the roles are reversed, as Tanizaki told Satō—it is the woman (Shunkin) who is disfigured and the man (Sasuke) who must respond. Again, the response contrasts with Barbara's. Sasuke is "as afraid of seeing her as Shunkin was of being seen" (72), perhaps because he cannot trust his love for her to survive the shock. Ultimately he transcends her disfigurement by sacrificing his own vision. As in *The Secret History*, the result is "complete love" and emotional fulfillment: "Always before, even while they were making love, they had been separated by the gulf between teacher and pupil. But now Sasuke felt that they were truly united, locked in a tight embrace" (74). Finally, and most significantly, both Barbara and Sasuke try to perpetuate the beloved's lost beauty. Barbara's attempt, by means of a statue, fails, but Sasuke succeeds by blinding himself and constructing an "imperishable ideal" to take the place of the tangible Shunkin.[15]

Sasuke's idealization of Shunkin is part of a larger tendency for the couple to create and inhabit a world of their own, increasingly detached from people and events around them. Their isolation, which is caused, perpetuated, and symbolized by their blindness, is particularly striking against the background of their times. Shunkin is born in 1829, Sasuke in 1825. Shunkin loses her sight in 1837, several years before the Tempō reform, and Sasuke in 1865, which is the year the couple's isolation becomes complete, but also the year the British minister Sir Harry Parkes arrived in Japan and only two years before the accession of the Meiji emperor and the collapse of the Tokugawa shogunate. Shunkin lives on to 1886 and Sasuke to 1907, which means that Sasuke lives through the promulgation of the Meiji Constitution, the Sino-Japanese War, and the Russo-Japanese War. Not one of these events leaves the slightest trace on the narrative. The more Japan emerges from Tokugawa seclusion, the more isolated Shunkin and Sasuke become. By spanning the turbulent years of the late Tokugawa and early Meiji, the setting of *A Portrait of Shunkin* demonstrates the degree to which Shunkin and Sasuke are unmindful of the outside world.

Current events would have made readers in 1933 sensitive to Shunkin's and Sasuke's isolation. Japan, with the rest of the world, was in an economic depression. "Reaction and aggression were in the air."[16] Memories of the Manchurian Incident of 1931 were still fresh, and it was in early 1933 that the ugly trends of the time found concrete representation in such events as the death in police custody of the proletarian writer Kobayashi Takiji (born 1903) and Japan's withdrawal from the League of Nations. Air raid drills began in August, just two months after *A Portrait of Shunkin* was published. As if to emphasize the distance between Sasuke's hermetic world and modern Japan, the narrator relates Shunkin's and Sasuke's graves to 1933 Osaka: "Here, high over the busiest industrial city of the Orient, over the innumerable tall buildings that pierce the evening haze, teacher and pupil lie together in their eternal sleep, bound by a mysterious fate. Osaka has changed almost beyond recognition since Sasuke's day, but these two stones still testify to his love for Shunkin" (5–6). The narrator of *Shunkin* also refers to an essay Tanizaki had published in 1932, mentions Satō Haruo, and quotes from a newspaper article published "on February 12 of this year (1933)."[17] In short, the narrative draws attention to the isolation of Shunkin and Sasuke by showing them to be oblivious to events that any reader would have known about, and reinforces the point with specific references to the Japan of the early 1930s.

One way the couple perfect their detachment is to perpetuate their relationship as teacher and pupil. Their refusal to marry, their rejection of their children, the appellations they use for each other (and insist that others use), and even the design of their gravestones all serve to fix these roles. In maintaining the "propriety of teacher and pupil" (*shitei no rei*) so assiduously, they go against the ordinary practice of their times. Sasuke insists that his pupils call him "Sasuke-san" rather than "Master" (*oshishō-san*, 13:553), "but this embarrassed them so much that they tried not to address him at all" (80). The narrative itself reinforces this anomaly by referring to Sasuke again and again as "Kengyō," his official title as a samisen master and one that Shunkin herself never attains. The narrative also provides constant reminders of the teacher-pupil relationship.[18] In short, there is a discrepancy between the public view, in which Sasuke is Kengyō, and his own private view, according to which he is merely Shunkin's pupil.

The most dramatic means that Sasuke chooses to complete and perpetuate his detachment from the outside world is to blind himself. His decision does not come on the spur of the moment. It is the culmination of years of empathy, even envy, for Shunkin's blindness. Before he begins to take samisen lessons from Shunkin, he practices being blind secretly at night in a closet:

> But Sasuke never felt inconvenienced by the darkness. . . . He was delighted to have found a place for himself in that dark world of hers. . . . In short, he wanted to suffer the same handicap as Shunkin, to share all he could of the life of the blind. At times he obviously envied them. And these attitudes in which he persisted since boyhood help to account for his own later blindness. It was something that had to happen.
>
> (22)

Blindness, when he finally achieves it, makes "this world into a paradise, where my mistress and I were alone together" (80).

Other Tanizaki characters cherish secret fantasies, but few go so far as Sasuke to attempt an ideal, private world of their own, and it is hard to think of any whose efforts are so successful. If we are to believe Sasuke (as the narrator says, "one hesitates to take Sasuke too literally" [81]), he and Shunkin live out their lives in bliss, and the secrecy of their private world is such that even the painstaking narrator cannot always penetrate it.

Shunkin and Sasuke are not equal partners in constructing and maintaining their ideal world, however. Shunkin inhabits this world, but Sasuke is the one who designs, executes, and maintains it. As early as 1933, Satō Haruo asserted that *A Portrait of Shunkin* is actually "A Portrait of Sasuke."[19] The truth of this will emerge gradually as the discussion continues. The first step is to examine the factor that ultimately makes the perfection of Sasuke's private world possible: his idealization of Shunkin. Only the man in the reeds, in *The Reed Cutter*, approaches Sasuke's success in surmounting the limitations of the flesh.

Sasuke's idealization of Shunkin is intimated early in the novella and by the end is well established as a principal theme. The narrator says near the beginning that Sasuke "seems to have seen Shunkin as a god" (13:498; my translation), and then, after describing Shunkin's photograph, speculates as follows:

> Was the picture of her which he carried in his memory in old age as faded as this photograph? Or did his imagination make up for a gradually failing memory? Did he create an image of another lovely woman, of one altogether different from the woman in the photograph?
>
> (9)

The answers to the second and third questions are affirmative. After Shunkin's disfigurement, Sasuke "closed his eyes to reality and leapt into the world of his imperishable ideal" (13:552; my translation), and "used the real Shunkin to call to mind the *ideal* Shunkin" (79).[20]

The religious metaphor reappears when Sasuke gazes at Shunkin for the first time after piercing his eyes. "As a god" has become more specific: "like the Buddha Amida."

> [A]ll he could detect was the pale, blurred image of her bandage-swathed face. But he had no thought of the bandages. It was his teacher's exquisite white face—as it had looked until only two months ago—that hovered before him in a circle of dim light, like the Buddha Amida, coming to lead a devout believer to the Pure Land.
>
> (13:548; translation adapted from Hibbett, p. 75.)

The "ideal Shunkin" in Sasuke's mind is far lovelier than the "real Shunkin" he has been able to see before: "It was only after I went blind that I realized how beautiful she was. . . . Why had I never before been so moved by her loveliness?" (81) His absorption in the ideal is so complete that he hardly notices when the "real Shunkin" is no longer with him: "As long as we remember them, we can see the dead in dreams; but for Sasuke, who saw his lover only in dreams even while she was still alive, it may have been hard to realize when the separation came" (83). The narrator concludes that Sasuke, after Shunkin's death, "created a Shunkin quite remote from the actual woman, yet more and more vivid in his mind" (84), thus confirming his speculation regarding the photograph. The unchanging, ideal image of Shunkin that Sasuke creates can be compared to Barbara's beautiful statue of her dead, disfigured husband, and to the ageless Oyū that the man in the reeds anticipates in *The Reed Cutter.* It is a reversal of the situation in Oscar Wilde's *Picture of Dorian Gray,* where the title character remains eternally youthful, while his portrait ages.[21]

Tanizaki emphasized the distinction between the outside world and Sasuke's ideal world when he commented, two years later, on the first film version of *A Portrait of Shunkin.* "If I were to make it into a film myself," he writes, "I would present a beautiful, fantasy-world Shunkin from the standpoint of Sasuke after he has blinded himself, and develop the story by juxtaposing this image with the real world" (22:321).

The reader's impression of Sasuke's ideal world is shaped by the language that it is presented in. The novella's beautiful, almost hypnotic prose style holds the reader in the warm embrace of the narrator. Especially toward the end, the reader feels like a child, snuggled in Grandfather's lap, half asleep, content and secure, listening to a story being told in a soothing voice. The style represents, as one critic has put it, "an attempt to express the reality of Sasuke's improbable psychology in the shadows of the language and the vagueness of the logic."[22] Another commentator likens the style's impact to the impact of the theater: "The reader is lured into a trance by the dreamlike fascination and intense stimulation of the story, but the moment he steps out of the theater, he is helpless before the bleak scenes of reality that press in upon him."[23]

The novella is divided into twenty-seven unnumbered sections, with no further division into paragraphs, even to set off dialogue. Punctuation is used sparingly. Sentences are long and, because there is little punctuation, often run together. The orthography of the first edition, which Tanizaki designed himself, includes a number of archaic variant *kana* forms, giving the printed page the look of an eighteenth- or early nineteenth-century book. Other stylistic features derive from the Japanese classics (such as *The Tale of Genji*), which ordinarily employed little or no punctuation; from Western stream-of-consciousness novels like *Ulysses;* and from the Irish novelist George Moore (1852–1933). In essays he wrote shortly after *A Portrait of Shunkin,* Tanizaki modestly implies that his style was an old man's surrender to Japanese tradition and to senescence. In fact, Tanizaki, like other twentieth-century novelists, was eager to experiment with different approaches and new forms. If some of his ideas came from the classics, others came from Western novelists, and he chose carefully, with specific effects in mind.

In 1934 Tanizaki wrote about the way he blends dialogue and narrative in *A Portrait of Shunkin:*

> I chose this form after studying the technique of George Moore in *Héloïse and Abélard* [1921] and later works, and of the classical Japanese novel from *The Tale of Genji* on. As everyone knows, it is hard to distinguish dialogue from narrative in the rainy-night passage of "The Broom Tree" [the second chapter] in the *Genji*, and hard to know who starts talking where, but the beauty of Japanese prose is most apparent in such passages. This intrigues me, and I have paid special attention to the links between narrative and dialogue. In *Quicksand* I accommodated the reader to the extent of providing quotation marks, but I did away with them in *The Reed Cutter.*[24]

Here is an example of Moore's technique:

> This is my study, said Fulbert, and the room on the other side of this wall, the room off the hall, is the room in which I have my meals. Supper is at eight. I suppose thou wilt have supper with me, Héloïse? Héloïse restrained a smile, and the words that rose to her lips were: I suppose I shall, unless I am going to bed supperless. Come and I'll show thee the house, for I see that thou hast an eye for a house, he continued, speaking like one who desires to please.[25]

In *Bunshō tokuhon* (A Reader on Style, 1934), Tanizaki points out that modern Japanese punctuation usage was adapted from that of the West. He contends, however,

> that Japanese prose does not require the use of a Western-style sentence structure, and so I make no attempt to employ punctuation in the Western manner. . . .
>
> In punctuating *A Portrait of Shunkin* as I did, my principal objectives were (1) to obscure the points of separation between sentences, (2) to extend the distance between breath-pauses, and (3) to achieve a feeling of lightness and weakness, like that of quick calligraphy in thin ink.
>
> (21:213, 215–216)[26]

Satō Haruo characterized the technique of *A Portrait of Shunkin* as "essentialism," in contrast to "Naturalistic realism."[27] One commentator has gone so far as to say that the style of *A Portrait of Shunkin* is the antithesis of the "trivialism" found in Proust's and Joyce's minute, realistic descriptions, and that it had a salutary effect on the Japanese literary world.[28] Ironically, though, Tanizaki's stated intention was "to find the form that would convey the greatest feeling of reality." He considered the "orthodox style of writing," with its "scene-building and dialogue," to be less realistic than "the drier elegance of the essay style."[29] "I hardly ever read the literary columns in the magazines" he admits, "because I find it tedious to watch the story totter through an elaborate design when the same material could be handled in a page or less of straightforward narrative." He concludes, "if we are concerned with awakening in the reader a sense of reality, then a plain, descriptive statement is most effective; and when the novel form is used, greater adroitness brings diminished plausibility."[30]

Even more important than prose style in Tanizaki's program to "convey the greatest feeling of reality" is the narrative situation he devised for *A Portrait of Shunkin. Shō* in the title *Shunkinshō* has been defined as "a critical commentary."[31] Like the narrator of *The Secret History of the Lord of Musashi*, the narrator of *Shunkin* is a scholarly antiquarian who has come across an old document (*The Life of Mozuya Shunkin*) and retells its story, filling in gaps with information from other sources and with his own surmises, assessing the reliability of his sources, and making tentative choices when his sources are contradictory or implausible. Little that the narrator says is definitive, but his questions "act as a device to cast over the somewhat fabulous and hallucinatory narrative a thin semblance of ordinary reality."[32] Skeptical comments from the narrator (e.g., "we can't be sure how objective Sasuke's version is") have a double effect. They plant in the reader's mind the possibility that Sasuke's version is unreliable and, at the same time, lend credibility to Sasuke's words by reassuring the reader that the narrator is scrupulous (even if he is not omniscient) and by inducing the reader to give Sasuke the benefit of the doubt.

A Portrait of Shunkin, like Akutagawa's famous story "Yabu no naka" (In a Grove, 1922) offers several perspectives on events—those of the narrator, *The Life of Mozuya Shunkin*, Sasuke, Shigizawa Teru, and the other sources—but provides no unqualified frame of reference. *A Portrait of Shunkin* requires the reader to participate more imaginatively than does a narrative that provides a straightforward perspective; and maximizing the reader's participation enhances plausibility. As another novelist has written about *Shunkin*, "withholding final judgments stimulates the reader's imagination more and gives rise to a sense of reality. It is the reader who provides the sense of reality."[33]

Tanizaki's doubts about "the need for psychological analysis, character portrayal, dialogue, and scene changes"[34] and his emphasis on "a feeling of reality" achieved by engaging the reader's imagination make *A Portrait of Shunkin* an unusually challenging work. There were complaints from the first that not enough was revealed about the characters' mentality. Just one year after *Shunkin* was published, Tanizaki responded, "To the criticism that I have not written about the psychology of Shunkin and Sasuke, I should like to respond with a question: what need is there to describe their psychology? Is it not clear from what I have written?"[35]

Several commentators with strongly held opinions might answer, "Yes, it is clear," but their opinions differ dramatically from one another. The most interesting controversy has been over the question, "Who disfigured Shunkin?" Until the late 1970s, most commentators unquestioningly accepted Sasuke's assertion, and the narrator's conclusion, that the culprit is an unidentified intruder. A few have assumed that Ritarō is the villain.[36] The first to cast a critical eye on Sasuke himself was the novelist Kōno Taeko, who wrote in 1976, "I count none other than Sasuke as yet another, particularly likely suspect, and envision a 'New Portrait of Shunkin.'"[37] Two years later, Nosaka Akiyuki, also a novelist, offered a revolutionary reading of the novella: "It was probably Sasuke who scalded Shunkin. The best means would probably have been to kill her, if his objective had been simply to possess her; but Sasuke chooses a method that lends itself to sensual gratification, as well."[38] Nosaka's hypothesis initiated a series of articles that flesh out the "Sasuke-as-culprit" theory or propound other interpretations.[39] After fifteen years, the controversy has died down, though no consensus has been reached.

The most important cause of ambiguity in *A Portrait of Shunkin* is the narrator's lack of authority. Conscientious as he is, the narrator of *Shunkin* simply cannot know exactly what happened, and he may sometimes be unwilling to reveal what he does know. Other sources of information, beyond *The Life of Mozuya Shunkin* and Shigizawa Teru, are hinted at but never identified. Who are they? How good is their information? The few instances in which the narrator does present definitive information stand out for their unambiguity. Examples are his description of the gravestones (he has seen and touched them) and the testimony of a friend who once heard Shunkin perform. On most subjects, the narrator says that he just does not know for sure. Should we believe him? Is there reason not to? He introduces a number of questions: Is Sasuke the father of Shunkin's child? Here, at least, the narrator provides a clear (if off-handed) answer. But what caused Shunkin's blindness? Several theories are offered, none of them convincing. Was she as good a dancer as she claimed? More than one interpretation is possible. Why does she agree to teach Sasuke? No satisfactory answer. Who disfigures Shunkin? The narrator speculates on all these questions but claims to lack definitive answers, and the reader forges ahead, tantalized by the obscurities and hoping for enlightenment.

A complicating factor in the narrator's uncertainty is the unreliability of his most important source, *The Life of Mozuya Shunkin.* The narrator makes it clear at the outset that the *Life* reflects Sasuke's point of view: "Although the text is written in the old-fashioned literary style and Sasuke himself is referred to in the third person, he undoubtedly supplied all the material and may well be regarded as the real author" (7). Immediately upon quoting from the *Life* for the first time, the narrator hints that Sasuke is unreliable: "Supposing that the source of this information was Sasuke, who seems to have seen Shunkin as a god, one hardly knows how much of it to believe" (13:498; translation adapted from Hibbett, p. 8). A few pages later, the narrator is more direct: "Sasuke's opinions are by no means to be trusted implicitly" (11); and when he presents Sasuke's first version of Shunkin's disfigurement and his own blindness, the narrator says flatly, "there is no denying that this account has been deliberately falsified" (69–70). But what about the instances when the narrator does *not* question Sasuke's version of events? Are they to be accepted at face value? Is Sasuke's second version of Shunkin's calamity, for example, more plausible than the first simply because the narrator does not question it? Only the reader can decide—but the reader must be conscious of the framework within which information is being provided.

The reader needs to be aware that the narrator has a tendency to identify with Sasuke. The narrator's behavior in the graveyard provides an early hint of his feelings: "After kneeling at Shunkin's grave for a moment, I ran my hand affectionately along the top of Sasuke's stone" (6). While the narrator's voice is distinguished from Sasuke's at first, their voices blend as the story progresses, particularly after the narrator begins to describe the origins of Sasuke's relationship with Shunkin. It is at this point that the narrator starts calling him Sasuke, instead of Kengyō (Master).[40] With the shift from "Kengyō" to "Sasuke," the narrator also shifts his perspective closer to Sasuke's. The narrative tends to become more subjective, and the narrator begins to make assertions that, while apparently objective, could only have originated with Sasuke's private perceptions. How are we to take, for example, the narrator's assertion that "He seemed to be no more than a hand to her" (18)? Seemed to whom? To Sasuke, of course. How does the narrator know? Presumably from the *Life*, authored by Sasuke. Does this assertion tell us more about Sasuke or about Shunkin? The reader's first response is to accept the narrator's (and Sasuke's) perspective and take the statement as evidence of Shunkin's coldness; but in fact it says nothing about Shunkin and much about Sasuke. The same is true of other assertions that seem at first to reveal something about Shunkin.

Again, the narrator tells us that "in the nude, her body was unexpectedly voluptuous. And she was dazzlingly fair—her skin kept its youthful gloss and freshness throughout her life" (45). The narrator is in no position to know this. He is speaking for Sasuke. Put another way, he has accepted Sasuke's point of view as his own. This being the case, it is difficult to accept without question a statement like, "As one learns more and more about Shunkin, one begins to realize how much trouble she gave Sasuke" (46). Thus the narrator himself, who has seemed so conscientious at first, turns out only to be less unreliable than Sasuke, for he presents as objective information about Shunkin material that actually reflects Sasuke's perception of Shunkin.

A close reading of the text, with special attention to the narrative situation, yields an unflattering image of Sasuke. He follows Shunkin everywhere "like a shadow" (6), attending to everything she does, "no matter how much she objected" (19). He even ministers to her in the toilet (though both English translations obscure this detail): "My teacher never washed her hands when she emerged from the toilet," says Shigizawa Teru, "because she never used her own hands when she relieved herself. Sasuke did everything for her" (13:525, my translation). In the process, Sasuke makes himself indispensable to Shunkin, but it is not clear that Shunkin welcomes all this attention.

Sasuke sounds like a pest. Worse, he is almost unbelievably self-centered. He is glad he has never seen Shunkin before her blindness, because "her face might later have seemed imperfect to him" (15). He prefers Shunkin to her sisters because she is blind, but he never feels sorry for her (16), even though, by Sasuke's own account, Shunkin considers blindness a terrible obstacle. "Sasuke said that she often told him her real talent was for dancing: those who praised her voice or her ability at the koto and samisen didn't know her true self—if only she could see, she would be a dancer" (11). But Sasuke is not interested in her "true self." He solipsistically dismisses the agony she has suffered at the hands of her attacker. "Now that I'm blind," he boasts, "it's as if nothing happened to you. Actually, it's anything but a misfortune for me—I've never had such a stroke of good luck" (76). When Shunkin loses her spirit after being attacked, Sasuke responds by concentrating more on his "ideal Shunkin" and turning away from the woman herself. "If Shunkin had actually changed in character because of her misfortune she would no longer have been Shunkin. He wanted to think of her as the proud, haughty girl of the past; otherwise, the beautiful Shunkin of his imagination would have been destroyed" (79). Finally, as we have seen, he withdraws from her so far that, when she dies, "it may have been hard [for him] to realize when the separation came" (83). The narrative provides, then, what Nosaka calls "the exhaustive depiction of a man's willfulness and egocentrism."[41]

There is less material for a clear picture of Shunkin. The narrative affords few objective glimpses of her, but when it does, the view differs from the perceptions that come filtered through Sasuke's subjectivity. First, there is Shunkin's photograph, which the narrator has seen, but his description is not what we might expect. "I can detect nothing more than the usual refinement of a lady from a well-to-do Osaka merchant family—beautiful, to be sure, but without any real individuality" (8). Even more significant, because it differs radically from the impression gained from Sasuke's point of view, is the narrator's revelation that "Shunkin is such a meek, gentle-looking woman that one feels a sense of compassion in her veiled eyes, as one would in those of the merciful goddess Kannon" (9). Are these impressions simply the result of a hazy photograph's deception? Not necessarily. "[A]s a child she was so gay and charming and vivacious, so considerate to those who served her, that she got along very well with people. She was on the best of terms with her brothers and sisters, and seemed to be the darling of the household" (10). Even in middle age "she was surprisingly pleasant; when invited to dinner, for instance, her whole manner was so gracious and appealing that no one would have taken her for the woman who, in her own home, tormented Sasuke or scolded and slapped her pupils" (54). This statement is particularly interesting, as it offers both an outside, objective view and Sasuke's private, subjective view of a Shunkin who "tormented" him.

The statement that "after losing her sight she became moody: she seemed almost taciturn, and seldom laughed" (17), should not be accepted uncritically. The year Shunkin loses her sight is also the year she meets Sasuke, who from the first (the narrator suggests) exerts a powerful influence on her: "Had she not become vaguely aware of his adoration and, young as she was, taken pleasure in it?" (17–18) What is more, "Sasuke disliked seeing her laugh" (17). Her moodiness may be caused not only by her blindness but also by a child's natural confusion over Sasuke's "adoration" and her own response to it. What of Shunkin's "stubbornness and willfulness"? There is no indication that she ever displays them to anyone but Sasuke, who "did his best to cater to these tendencies in her" (19). Is she naturally sadistic? Probably not, concludes the narrator. Her harsh treatment of Sasuke is a child's "inevitable" imitation of her own master's practice (31), and her treatment of her pupils is no worse than that of other teachers of traditional arts. There is, in short, no objective confirmation of Sasuke's perception that Shunkin—the real Shunkin—is a difficult, demanding, sadistic woman. The "ideal Shunkin" has all these traits, but the ideal Shunkin and the real Shunkin are not the same person. It is instructive to recall the narrator's comment in *The Secret History of the Lord of Musashi:* "a man who has masochistic sexual appetites . . . is apt to construct fantasies in which his female partner conforms to his own perverse specifications; and so the woman, in most cases, is not at all the pitiless creature she is made out to be."[42]

The nature of Shunkin's relationship with Sasuke is suggested by the elaborate symbolism of her birds. Shunkin's nightingales are trained by a "teaching bird" (*shishō,* "teacher," the same word used for Shunkin by her pupils), are particular about their food, and are kept in a cloaked cage, where they are fussed over by Shunkin and her servants. The narrator reinforces the parallel between Shunkin and her nightingales by saying that she "conceived the idea for [her finest composition] while she was listening to Tenko," and "whenever Shunkin played it Tenko sang out joyously, straining its voice to rival the beauty of her samisen" (83). If Shunkin's nightingale is an emblem for Shunkin herself, what emerges is the image of a woman caged and cut off from the outside world at the whim of, and for the pleasure of, the man who fusses over, feeds, and bathes her. One is reminded of Jōji and Naomi. "Since coming under my charge," Jōji boasts, ". . . she'd become a truly radiant, vivacious little bird, and the enormous atelier was her cage."[43] Shunkin's larks, on the other hand, soaring high in the sky to sing, suggest her longing for freedom—from blindness, from confinement, from Sasuke. When her lark soars up and never returns, Shunkin, too, makes her final escape: she dies.

Viewed from this perspective, Sasuke looks a lot like other Tanizaki men. Seikichi (in "Shisei" [The Tattooer, 1910]) uses the artistry of his tattoos to mold a young geisha into a sadistic monster, and then eagerly becomes her first victim. Jōji, too (whether intentionally or not), transforms the ingenuous Naomi into a willful tyrant and becomes her slave. The Lord of Musashi tries to corrupt his wife in the same way and fantasizes about a cruel woman by whom he could be manipulated. Like these men, Sasuke molds a woman to dominate his fantasy life as his "ideal woman," and when he has maneuvered her right to where he wants her, he throws himself at her feet. When she has outlived her usefulness, he creates an idealized mental image to replace her.

In conclusion: Sasuke and Shunkin live in a private, ideal realm of their own, where they are oblivious to the world outside. Transcending even this private world, Sasuke constructs an ideal Shunkin, distinct from his flesh-and-blood lover. The hypnotic style of the writing lures the reader into Sasuke's dream world and into accepting Sasuke's point of view. Efforts to identify Shunkin's attacker have been fruitless. Chiba believes that a profitable next step in *Shunkin* criticism would be to study *Shunkin* as an alternative to the orthodox novelistic form inherited from nineteenth-century Europe.[44]

SIX

The Makioka Sisters

The Makioka Sisters, Tanizaki's longest and most famous work, has been called "the greatest cosmopolitan novel since the Meiji Restoration."[1] Most of it was written during the Second World War, when Tanizaki, prevented by the government from publishing, could devote his energy over a period of years to this nostalgic evocation of wealthy merchant-class life between Kobe and Osaka in the late 1930s.

Tanizaki preferred to let ideas for his novels brew for years before he put brush to paper, and this was the case with *The Makioka Sisters.* Though he wrote the novel between 1942 and 1948, he seems to have had something like it in mind almost ten years earlier, when he described his plans to Satō Haruo. Satō recalled:

> [The novel] would be about the world of stockbrokers, the segment of society that most sensitively registers each and every worldwide upheaval. The hero would be someone who had grown up as a student in Tokyo and left to join the ranks of merchants in the Osaka stock market. At times the author would have him mouthing arguments like a typical Tokyo man fresh out of school, spouting intellectual theories about society, civilization, and the like. Again, he would portray him completely at home with the lively and picturesque Osaka dialect, thinking like an Osaka merchant, talking and behaving with the mentality of one born and bred in Osaka. And of course scattered throughout would be the author's own observations on the mores of Tokyo and Osaka society—some them already expressed in his essays—and piquant revelations about the pleasure quarters or the

> inner chambers, in which he would no doubt give full play to his wide interest in such matters.[2]

Explaining to Satō why he had abandoned the project, Tanizaki said, "First of all, it just isn't like me, so I've decided against it."[3] Nevertheless, he continued to develop his ideas. The 1934 fragment *Natsugiku* (Summer Chrysanthemums) appears to have been a start at something along these lines, but Tanizaki broke it off after only two installments. Revising his plans, he envisioned a novel even longer than *The Makioka Sisters* turned out to be, tentatively called "Sankan shion" (Three Cold Days, Four Warm, i.e., Early Spring). It was to be a complex picture of the "corrupt and decadent" upper-class society of Ashiya and Shukugawa (23:364), and to portray a broad range of characters (rather than just one family), including the "rich, idle women who live between Osaka and Kobe" (23:237). The increasing intensity of Japan's war with China and the vigilance of government censors led Tanizaki, however, "drastically to narrow the scope" of the novel and omit most of the "decadence" (23:237): "In retrospect this is regrettable, to be sure, but had I not been forced into idleness by the storms of war, I would not have been able to devote six years to a single work; and if most of the decadence had to be omitted and the beautiful emphasized, that was the inescapable fate of a novel born of war and peace" (22:363–364).

After his first modern-Japanese translation of *The Tale of Genji*, completed in 1938, Tanizaki published little, and no new fiction at all, during the four years he devoted to planning *The Makioka Sisters.* He offered a few examples of the care he took in his preparations: "Since the events in the novel were inseparable from the times—the period of internal deterioration, shall we say, or the period that produced various sideslips as Japan was preparing for war—I had to make a chronological table with the complete story line on one side and the corresponding external events on the other. For example, before I could let my characters hail a cab, I had to find out whether cabs were available at that time and place, and how much the fare was. When I sent a character to Tokyo, I wondered whether third-class sleeping cars had not been discontinued by that time. I might have made some serious errors if I had failed to investigate these details one by one" (22:364). Shortly after completing

The Makioka Sisters, he recalled, "When I was young I sometimes started writing before my ideas had taken shape completely, and consequently I often found myself in a difficult position; but in the case of *The Makioka Sisters,* I began writing only after I had made a detailed outline" (23:238).[4]

The first eight chapters of *The Makioka Sisters* were published in the New Year's, 1943, edition of *Chūō Kōron.* In the same issue, the veteran poet and novelist Shimazaki Tōson (1872–1943) began serialization of a new novel, *Tōhō no mon* (Gate of the East). (Tōson died in August, before he could complete the third chapter.) The simultaneous publication of new works by two celebrated writers attracted the attention of the public and, naturally, of the censors. Chapters 9 through 13 of *The Makioka Sisters* appeared in the March, 1943, issue, and the June issue was to carry chapters 14 through 19. Tanizaki had planned to suspend publication at that point (23:191), but the censors beat him to it by bullying the editors at *Chūō Kōron* into discontinuing serialization before the June issue was printed.[5]

Tanizaki went on writing and in July, 1944, published a private edition in 248 copies of book 1, which he distributed among friends. The government was not pleased, and the police warned Tanizaki not to publish any more of the novel, in any format. Nevertheless, he continued to write steadily through the war and after. Until the war ended, he always kept the manuscript in a bag at his side, so that he could carry it with him whenever he had to take refuge in a bomb shelter. Book 2 was completed in December, 1944, and book 3, delayed by the effects of high blood pressure, in 1948.

The title *Sasameyuki* is a poetic word meaning "lightly falling snow." It was rarely used before the novel was published. Tanizaki wrote that he chose *Sasameyuki* as the title in preference to *San shimai* (Three Sisters), with the intention of making Yukiko the central character (23: 237, 365). (The Chinese character for *yuki*—snow—is the same in both.)[6] The snow of the title is figurative, as snow never falls in the novel. One would not expect to see snow in Ashiya, where a mild climate prevails; but more to the point, there is scarcely any winter in the narrative and, even when the time and setting are right (as in January, 1941, when the family visits Count Mimaki in Saga), snow is not mentioned. The title evokes instead the image of light snow and, by conventional extension, of cherry petals fluttering to the ground as the blossom season passes its peak.[7]

A fondness for snow as a metaphor for cherry blossoms goes back at least to the *Kokin wakashū* (Collection of Ancient and Modern Japanese Poems, compiled ca. 905), the anthology that established the tone and diction for all subsequent court poetry.

On Seeing the Cherry Blossoms Scatter at Urin'in

Sakura chiru hana no tokoro wa haru nagara
yuki zo furitsutsu kiegate ni suru

Here where the cherry petals flutter to the ground spring has come and yet
Snow is falling on and on and shows no signs of melting.

(by the Priest Sōku; *Kokinshū* no. 75)

On Cherry Blossoms Scattering

Yuki to nomi furu dani aru o
sakurabana ika ni chire to ka kaze no fuku ran

If they must fall let them fall gently like snow,
But see how the wind commands the cherry blossoms to scatter!

(by Ōshikōchi no Mitsune; *Kokinshū* no. 86)

Tanizaki uses the conceit in several poems he composed concurrently with *The Makioka Sisters:*

Yamazato wa sakura fubuki ni akekurete
hana naki niwa mo hana zo chirishiku[8]

The mountain village rises and retires to a cherry blizzard—
even this flowerless garden is carpeted with fallen flowers.

(16:75)

Yuki to bakari sode ni chirikishi hana narade
otsuru konoha zo sakura narikeru

Scattering like snowflakes and clinging to my sleeves—
They are not blossoms but leaves falling from the cherry trees!

(16:79)

By referring to the pink-blossoming trees at the Heian Shrine, the second of Tanizaki's poems demonstrates how completely the conventional association between cherry blossoms and snow has lost any connection with sensory experience. The *Kokinshū* poems are about the white, Yoshino variety:

Miyoshino no yamabe ni sakeru sakurabana
yuki ka to nomi zo ayamatarekeru

Blossoming on the hills of noble Yoshino—cherry flowers—
And I was convinced that I was seeing snow!

(by Ki no Tomonori; *Kokinshū* no. 60)

In the imagistic vocabulary of Japanese poetry, then, snow (in a spring poem) evokes cherry blossoms. Cherry blossoms, in turn, are a common metaphor for ephemeral beauty, since they bloom for only a short time and the flowers are easily spoiled by wind and rain. Thus the Makiokas, too, "had the anxiety of the ancients over the weather, anxiety which had once seemed to Sachiko merely conventional. With each breeze and shower their concern for the cherries would grow" (86).[9] For Yukiko, who is blessed with "the beauty, fragile and elegant, of the sheltered maiden of old, the maiden *who had never known the winds of the world*" (35, emphasis added), the beautiful but fragile cherry blossom is as appropriate an emblem as "lightly falling snow." Significantly, the symbolism stressed by the Japanese government, which associated the cherry blossom with brave, beautiful warriors facing death in battle, has no place in *Sasameyuki*.

Some readers guessed, and Tanizaki confirmed, that the sisters are modelled after the author's wife Matsuko and her sisters (18:288–289). Sachiko corresponds to Mrs. Tanizaki; Tsuruko, Yukiko, and Taeko to her sisters Asako, Shigeko, and Nobuko, respectively; and Etsuko to Mrs. Tanizaki's daughter Emiko. There are models for some of the lesser characters, as well. Yukiko's fiancé Mimaki corresponds to Shigeko's husband Watanabe Akira, whom she married on April 29, 1941, the date of Yukiko's marriage in the novel. O-haru resembles one of the Tanizaki's maids; and Okubata Kei-boy seems to be modelled after Mrs. Tanizaki's first husband, Nezu Seitarō, who had an affair with his sister-in-law Nobuko. Teinosuke occupies Tanizaki's position in the family, but he cannot be identified with Tanizaki as confidently as the sisters can be with their counterparts. Teinosuke's relationship with Sachiko is fundamentally different from Tanizaki's with Matsuko; and the narrator's perspective is carefully distanced from Teinosuke's, as though the author were doing his best to prevent his readers—or himself—from identifying Teinosuke with Tanizaki.

Not surprisingly, much of the action of the novel is based on events in the lives of Tanizaki and his family in the late 1930s. Mrs. Tanizaki said that "almost everything we did during that period turns up in *The Makioka Sisters.*"[10] She seems to be referring, however, not to the major incidents of the novel, but to the embellishments—the memorable but, taken individually, inconsequential details that collectively produce a convincing picture of life. She specifically mentions Etsuko's composition about the rabbit's ear (I:8), seeing a hotel room reflected on the surface of a thermos bottle, her dream of glass and chinaware shattering, and her bout with bed bugs at the Nara Hotel (all in III:25).

The last three details can be found among the contents of two notebooks Tanizaki used from 1938 to 1943 to record impressions and events.[11] Of the fifty-two published entries, part or all of twenty-five actually appear in the novel, most of them modified. For example, Taeko's comments on how geisha eat (II:3) were actually made not by one of the sisters but by one Yagi Tsuyako in a conversation with Mrs. Tanizaki. Similarly, Itani's conversation with Sachiko about efficient modern housewives, at the *miai* with Segoshi (I:11), is a synthesis of two separate reports from Mrs. Tanizaki about her friends Mrs. Suguro and Mrs. Nango. The account of the sisters and Etsuko being aroused by spiders among their fireflies (III:6) is based on a scene enacted by strangers and observed by Tanizaki. The memorable dinner with the Kyrilenkos (I:17) closely follows an entry describing dinner with the Simonoff family. There were several visits with the Simonoffs. At one, the sisters were unable to finish everything on their plates and (as they do in the visit narrated in the novel) passed the excess to the Simonoffs' dog Prince; but their deception was exposed when Prince threw up on the floor. One can understand why Tanizaki chose not to include this inelegant detail in *The Makioka Sisters*, but the notes include other vignettes that he could have used effectively. For example: "Whenever it rains, Ashiya Station is crowded with people carrying umbrellas, there to meet the trains. You can see all sorts of people—young wives, maidservants, matrons, houseboys, old handymen."[12]

Of the notebook entries that did not find their way into *The Makioka Sisters*, the most significant is a long, harrowing account of Mrs. Tanizaki's 1939 abortion, which is transformed in the novel into Sachiko's 1938 miscarriage. Tanizaki no doubt had personal reasons for making this change; but it also accords with his decision to leave out the Russian dog's indiscretion and suggests a desire to present, at least in book 1, as beautiful a world as possible—an idealized world.

The events in *The Makioka Sisters* are nevertheless inseparable from the times, as Tanizaki said. A rough count yields twenty-seven references to world events—the "China Incident," Hitler's activities in Europe, the bombing of London, and so on. The sisters read the newspapers. If they seem insufficiently concerned about international developments, they are little different from their contemporaries in the West. A review of *1939: In the Shadow of War* reminds us that in Europe, too, "then, as now, many people preferred to ignore the events that would soon change their lives forever," because, for one thing, "the momentous . . . is often overshadowed by the momentary."[13] It is natural that the sisters are more concerned with finding a husband for Yukiko and with the family's reputation than they are with the ugly news from abroad. *The Makioka Sisters*, like *1939*, "succeeds brilliantly in conveying the texture of daily life poised on the brink of an abyss unimagined even by the most cleareyed, hardheaded, and pessimistic."[14] The reader knows, however—and the author knew—what lay in the sisters' future, after Yukiko's wedding in April, 1941, and this knowledge gives rise to "the premonition of the end of an era" that "broods darkly over the novel."[15] For all but a reader ignorant (or forgetful) of history, *The Makioka Sisters* is haunted by the ghosts of Pearl Harbor, the Tokyo fire bombings, Hiroshima and Nagasaki, and the Occupation.

The Makioka Sisters is not a chronicle of Tanizaki's world from 1936 to 1941, however. Much of what happens in the novel is fabricated. The misadventures of the youngest sister, for example, are exaggerated and fictionalized, particularly in book 3. The account of the flood, too, is largely fictional. There was a disastrous flood in the Kobe area in 1938, but Tanizaki, having been in Tokyo at the time, based his account on second-hand reports, photographs, and his imagination.[16] Had there never been a flood, it is unlikely that Tanizaki would have invented one, and to that extent it is true that the flood is there because it happened. More important is that the flood is a crucial vehicle for developing the characters of Taeko and Itakura, Teinosuke, Oharu, Sachiko, Okubata, and Mrs. Stolz, and serves as a central metaphor and a structural turning point on which the entire novel pivots.

The Makioka Sisters is as carefully structured as anything Tanizaki wrote. It contains several recurring cycles that, taken together, signal inevitable and universal decline against the background of the world's slide into war. The repeated narration of certain activities—expeditions to see the cherry blossoms and marriage negotiations being the most significant—is analogous to incremental repetition in the ballad. That is, the changes that occur in each repetition draw attention to themselves and form a pattern.

There is a pattern of decline in Yukiko's successive marriage negotiations, for example. The Makioka family turns down Segoshi's proposal, the first in the novel, for a good reason: there is a strain of insanity in Segoshi's family. Yukiko rejects the second suitor, Nomura, for less compelling reasons: he looks older than he is and he insensitively shows her a photograph of his dead wife. The Makiokas do not even have a chance to reject the third candidate, Sawazaki. He wastes no time telling the matchmaker that he is not interested in Yukiko. Dr. Hashidera, the fourth candidate, is even harsher. Though initially interested in Yukiko, after getting to know her better he rejects her for being "spineless, quivering, [and] old-fashioned" (413). In the course of these four negotiations, the family has gone from the lofty rejection of mediocre candidates to ignominious rejection by attractive ones. In the end, thanks to the extraordinary efforts of their friend Itani, a fairly good match is found. Attractive as he is, however, Mimaki might well have been rejected by the Makiokas in earlier, prouder days. His pedigree is attractive to the Makiokas, but in fact, as the illegitimate son of a Kyoto viscount—in other words, the dubious offspring of a moribund aristocracy—he embodies the decline of the old order.

The cherry-blossom excursions to Kyoto are another illustration of this pattern. Being "a fixed annual observance" (85), they are associated with the calendar of ritual observances perpetuated by generations of Kyoto courtiers, priests, and townspeople. Thus the blossoms are more than simply a beautiful sight—going to see them makes the Makiokas participants in the great tradition:

> All these hundreds of years, from the days of the oldest poetry collections, there have been poems about cherry blossoms. . . . How very ordinary the poems had seemed to Sachiko when she read them as a girl, but now she knew, as well as one could know, that grieving over fallen cherry blossoms was more than a fad or a convention.
>
> (85)

In the yearly excursions Sachiko finds both a disturbing reminder of the passage of time and the reassurance that comes with repeating the same activity again and again. Every detail of the outing is ritualized. One year the sisters have had their picture taken in a certain spot, and "ever since, they had made it a point to stand under the same tree and look out over the pond, and have their picture taken. Sachiko knew too that in the hedge that lined the path there would be a camellia loaded with crimson blossoms. She never forgot to look for it" (87–88). Any variation in the routine makes Sachiko uneasy. "Teinosuke had rebelled the year before and taken them instead to the Brocade Bridge [near Hiroshima]; but Sachiko had been restless afterwards, as though she had forgotten something. She complained that spring did not feel like spring, and finally took Teinosuke off to Kyoto in time for the late cherries at Omuro [in Kyoto]" (86).

The cherry blossom itinerary given in chapter 19 of book 1 is a *michiyuki*, a poetic litany of sights and impressions of a journey (we have seen that *Arrowroot* has a similar section): "They climbed the embankment of Osawa Pond . . . , and went on past the temple gates—the Temple of the Great Awakening, the Temple of Clean Coolness, the Temple of the Heavenly Dragon—to arrive at the Bridge of the Passing Moon . . ." (88; translator's interpolations deleted). The proper names in this passage—Ōsawanoike, Daikakuji, Seiryōji, Tenryūji, Togetsukyō—serve as cues to the informed reader, who will almost unconsciously provide images and literary and historical associations to go with them. Like the other place names in the chapter, they evoke the history of Kyoto literature and the court culture that engendered it, and so link the novel and the Makiokas to that culture.

A central aspect of court culture was a keen awareness of the changes wrought by time. The seasons come and go; one spring is much like another; but the seasons mock us, because we cannot remain the same. This poem by Ki no Tomonori (ninth century) is a representative expression of the sentiment:

> Iro mo ka mo onaji mukashi ni sakuramedo
> toshi furu hito zo aratamarikeru
>
> Their color and scent must be the same as when the cherries bloomed before,
> But being human I grow old and I have changed.
>
> (*Kokinshū* no. 57)

The sisters share this traditional awareness. "For Sachiko there was, besides pleasant sorrow for the cherry blossoms, sorrow for her sisters and the passing of their youth. She wondered whether each excursion might not be her last with Yukiko" (86). The fact that Yukiko is with her again this year—that the ritual has not changed—is an ironic reminder that Yukiko is a year older and still unmarried:

> All was well, they had come again to the cherries in full bloom. There was a feeling of relief, and a hope that next year they might be as fortunate, and for Sachiko, at least, the thought that even if she herself stood here next year, Yukiko might be married and far away. The flowers would come again, but Yukiko would not. It was a saddening thought, and yet it contained almost a prayer that, for Yukiko's sake,

> she might indeed no longer be with them. Sachiko had stood under these same trees with these same emotions the year before and the year before that, and each time she had found it hard to understand why they should still be together. She could not bear to look at Yukiko.
>
> (89)

The cherry-blossom excursion is, then, a chance to look back and to look forward, to reaffirm the family's continuity with its own past and with Japanese tradition, and to measure changes that have or have not taken place.

A pattern of decline emerges from the descriptions of the five cherry excursions in the novel. The first, that of 1937, from which the passages above are taken, is the happiest and establishes the norm that later excursions are to be measured against. Sachiko, Yukiko, and Taeko all take part (Tsuruko, the eldest, is never included in these outings), as well as Teinosuke and Etsuko. These five are the full complement. The weather and timing are perfect. The Makiokas can take their time as they go through the ritual, step by step.

None of the subsequent expeditions is as successful. The second (1938, at the end of book 1) is marred by the memory of Sachiko's miscarriage of a month before: "Even among the cherry-viewing crowds, Sachiko wept a little each time she passed someone with a baby. Rather upset, Teinosuke took her home with the others on Sunday night" (150). The third excursion (in 1939) is the last to include all three sisters. It could have been developed into a pleasant interlude of harmony among the family members, coming as it does amidst Taeko's difficulties with Okubata and Itakura, but a harmonious interlude has come already in the previous chapter, when the sisters visit their favorite sushi shop (II:30). The blossom expedition is passed over in one sentence as the narrative rushes ahead to a lurid description of Etsuko's scarlet fever. The following year (1940) Taeko, bedridden with dysentery, is unable to accompany the family on the fourth excursion, which is in any case "quiet and wholly without ostentation" because of the "national crisis" (458). The fifth excursion, that of 1941, is the only one since 1937 to be described in any detail. There is no joy in it, despite the family's pleasure over Yukiko's impending marriage. The timing is wrong, the sense of crisis is stronger than ever, the excursion is rushed, and Taeko—secretly ensconced in a maternity hospital—is absent:

> Time passed; the cherry blossoms were beginning to fall. . . . Caught by the austerity edicts, they were unable to have new wedding kimonos dyed, and finally had to have the Kozuchiya hunt up old ones. That month rice rationing began. Kikugorō was not making his usual spring visit to Osaka, and they had to be satisfied with an even quieter cherry viewing than the year before. But it was an annual rite, and summoning up their determination and taking care to dress as unobtrusively as possible, they made a one-day trip to Kyoto on Sunday the thirteenth.
>
> (526)

Significantly, the itinerary is not only abbreviated but also reversed from its normal order:

> After a look at the weeping cherries in the Heian Shrine, they rushed out to the western suburbs and went through the form of seeing the cherries there. This year they did without their party at the Gourd Restaurant. Taeko again was missing. The four of them spread a sad little lunch by Ōzawa Pond and had a rather solemn drink of cold saké from the lacquer cups, and when the excursion was over they hardly knew what they had seen.
>
> (526–527)

The outing has deteriorated into an empty formality, a desperate attempt by Sachiko and Yukiko to reaffirm some kind of continuity in their increasingly difficult lives. It fails precisely because it is unlike earlier excursions.

There is a turning point in the overall pattern of decline: the flood of July, 1938. The two cherry excursions before the flood are the happiest; the first after the flood is almost forgotten in the general concern over Etusko's scarlet fever. Similarly, it is the Makiokas who break off marriage negotiations before the flood, but in the first *miai* after the flood (Sawazaki's) Yukiko receives her first rejection. The function of the flood as a turning point is reinforced by the typhoon in Tokyo two months later. The members of the family who have been least affected by the flood—Sachiko, Yukiko, and Etsuko—suffer the most in the typhoon. Together, the flood and the typhoon shake the entire family—

and the entire country, represented by Kobe and Tokyo, in western and eastern Japan. The storms sweep away the elegant spirit and harmony that had characterized the Makiokas' lives. The rituals continue, but their observance is increasingly mechanical, empty, and even humiliating. Ultimately, the flood and typhoon symbolize the difficulties that complicate and disrupt the lives of the Makiokas (and of all Japanese) and speed their decline.

The illnesses that pervade *The Makioka Sisters* can also be seen as symbols of decline. Like the wind that scatters the cherry blossoms, disease signifies evanescence, and, as it reminds the characters and the reader of the body's vulnerability, disease is representative of an anxiety that runs through the novel.[17] The increasing severity of illnesses and problems relating to pregnancy in *The Makioka Sisters* follows the pattern of decline-in-repetition that is also at work in the cherry excursions and marriage negotiations. In book 1, the sisters have vitamin-B injections, Sachiko is troubled by jaundice, and Etsuko has beriberi and nervous prostration. The worst medical problem is Sachiko's miscarriage. Matters are more serious in book 2. Saku, the dance teacher, dies from uremic poisoning. Etsuko contracts scarlet fever, a contagious disease potentially far more serious than her earlier problems. Itakura suffers from a papillary infection and dies, prematurely and in excruciating pain, of gangrene. In book 3, Taeko nearly dies of dysentery and, a year later, suffers terribly through more than twenty hours of labor pains, only to lose the child because of a blunder by the attending physician. The contrast with Sachiko's miscarriage is obvious, and of the several deaths in the novel, the death of Taeko's baby is the saddest, the one that most engenders feelings of futility and despair.

In the end, even Yukiko, the healthiest of them all, suffers from diarrhea on the eve of her wedding. It is difficult not to see this final irony as broadly symbolic—not only of Yukiko's misgivings about marriage and about going to Tokyo, but also of the far more drastic problems that will soon face Yukiko and her sisters. Historical irony lies thick on the last pages of *The Makioka Sisters*. By April, 1941, less than eight months before Pearl Harbor and less than a year before the first bombing raid on Tokyo, Taeko has moved in with her future husband, O-haru's family has found her a husband, the Makioka's cat safely bears kittens, and a date is set for Yukiko's wedding. "Thus the future was settled," says the narrator, but we know better; and Sachiko's regret over Yukiko's engagement, the fact that Yukiko is headed for Tokyo to be wed on a patriotic holiday, and finally Yukiko's diarrhea, all bode ill for the future.

In the face of their own decline and the deterioration of the world situation, the Makiokas seek refuge in secrecy, which they require to preserve a certain *yutori*—space or latitude, a sort of calm in the storm—for themselves and their family. As the psychiatrist Takeo Doi has written, "In order to have *yutori* it is necessary to keep secret what it is that is most important to oneself. Otherwise one's freedom is lost, and one is no longer able to create something to spare when it is needed. There are no blank spaces or free time to fill, and one can no longer produce them."[18]

Yutori assumes concrete form as the garden at Ashiya. The garden is first mentioned in April, 1937. Yukiko has just learned that a marriage proposal from Mr. Nomura has come a month before. Yukiko appears to be upset with Sachiko for not telling her sooner, but it may be that the reason for her distress is being forced to think about marriage at all. She gazes down into the garden: the lawn, flower beds, dry lake, lilac, cherry, plane and sandalwood trees, syringa, and *yamabuki* spread in a panorama beneath her. Under the plane tree the children are playing house:

> "This is the father," said Rosemarie, taking up a doll in her left hand. "And this is the mother." She pressed the faces together, and there was a resounding smack. Rosemarie seemed to be providing the sound effects. "The baby came." She took a baby doll from the skirts of the "mother." "Baby came, baby came," she repeated happily.
>
> . . . Yukiko smiled on and on as she watched the play.
>
> (84–85)

A year later, in March, 1938, Sachiko observes Yukiko strolling through the garden, just as Yukiko has observed the children at play. As Yukiko moves from flower to flower, Sachiko knows "well enough without seeing her face what Yukiko was thinking: that she would soon be called back to Tokyo, and that she hated to leave spring in this garden behind" (147). This time the vignette comes after an even more upsetting experience, Sachiko's miscarriage and the disastrous *miai* with Nomura.

Sachiko herself hurries to the garden as soon as the flood of July, 1938, is over:

> As the sun came out, Sachiko went down from the terrace into the garden. Two white butterflies were dancing over the lawn, which was greener and fresher for the rain. Among the weeds between the sandalwood and the lilac a pigeon was fishing for something in the puddles. The tranquil scene carried not a hint that there had been a flood.
> (180)

Not only does Sachiko look to the garden for solace, but the garden itself has only been made more appealing by the rain that caused the flood. Before long, Yukiko strolls in the garden again, immediately after returning from Tokyo. Again the children are playing, and again the scene ends with Yukiko laughing as she watches. (The last sentence of the chapter involves an untranslatable pun, the cause of Yukiko's laughter, and is omitted from the translation [202].)

The garden is described yet again in September, 1938, just after Sachiko has returned from Tokyo, where she has been terrified by the typhoon and shocked by Okubata's letter. Again the garden plants are enumerated: hibiscus, *hagi*, sandalwood and plane trees, the lawn.

> These last two or three days she had felt an intense affection for the familiar garden. It was good to go away now and then. Possibly because she was not used to travelling, she felt that she had been away at least a month. She remembered how Yukiko treasured every minute, how she would walk through the garden, stopping here and there, when she had to go back to Tokyo. Yukiko was not the only child of Osaka, Sachiko knew.
> (243)

Sachiko returns to the garden in March, 1940, to calm herself after Yukiko's exasperating behavior on the telephone with Hashidera: "Angrier and angrier the longer she looked at her sister, Sachiko turned abruptly and started downstairs. She went out to the terrace and on into the garden" (412). Finally, the garden serves literally as a retreat for Teinosuke, who uses a cottage in the garden as his study; for Sachiko, when she needs to make a private telephone call; and for Etsuko when she is quarantined with scarlet fever.

The first time the Ashiya garden is described, it is juxtaposed to the main house—Tsuruko's house—in Osaka:

> For all its being rather small, the garden had in it two or three old native pines, and beyond the hedge it gave way to the hills of the Rokkō chain, off to the north and west. Yukiko always felt that she had come to life again when she was back in Ashiya after four or five days in the Osaka house.
>
> (84)

(We must make a distinction here between "Osaka" and "the Osaka house." Yukiko is a "child of Osaka"—that is, of the city and its distinctive culture—but she is uncomfortable with her sister Tsuruko, who lives first in the Osaka house and later in Tokyo.) A later description of the Ashiya garden echoes the first, but this time juxtaposes the garden with Tokyo, and the contrast is much greater:

> This was a most unremarkable little garden, but even here, smelling the pines, looking at the mountains and the clear sky, [Sachiko] thought that there could be no finer place to live than the suburbs of Osaka. How unpleasant Tokyo was, how dusty, gray, pushing.
>
> (243)

And Tsuruko's house in Tokyo has no garden at all. Between these two descriptions, Yukiko savors every moment in the Ashiya garden as she waits "in dread" for the call to return to Tokyo (147), and then heads straight for the garden the moment she has returned (201).

For both Sachiko and Yukiko, then—but especially for Yukiko—the garden is a soothing retreat from marriage proposals, Sachiko's miscarriage, flood and typhoon, distressing news, quarrels, and Tokyo. Each time we see Yukiko in the garden she is rejoicing to be in Ashiya and either relieved to be back or dreading her impending trip to Tokyo. The litany of flowers that recurs in each garden scene is analogous to the fixed routine of the cherry blossom excursions—the repetition of familiar names and activities produces the feeling of security that Yukiko needs. Sachiko has even had a cherry planted in the garden, so that they could "go cherry viewing at home" (84). Though the tree does not cooperate by blossoming to their satisfaction, its presence in the garden represents an attempt to bring the most pleasing aspects of the outside world inside the garden, where the family can enjoy them safely. The garden is also cosmopolitan, harboring foreign plants like syringa and lilac, and serving as a common ground where Etsuko plays with Rosemarie, and Sachiko chats with Mrs. Stolz.

The hominess of the garden is reinforced by the children at play in it. Completely absorbed, unaware that they are being watched, they are secure and at peace with the world. Yukiko smiles and laughs as she watches them, vicariously re-experiencing her own childhood and, for the moment, putting her problems and thoughts of marriage out of her mind. We know from other passages that Yukiko has an exceptionally strong rapport with Etsuko, and she hopes that if she marries someone with children, they will be little girls (19). Psychologically, Yukiko is still a child herself, every bit as spoiled and willful as Etsuko; and her desire to stay with her sisters at Ashiya, unmarried, strolling in the garden, watching the children at play, is a desire to remain in a state of eternal childhood.

Teinosuke's relationship with the garden might appear to be rather different, in view of the problems he has with birds, bees, the lawn, and the Hirado lilies; but he draws attention to another way the garden can be seen as a secure microcosm. Though he labors with mixed success, his chores are a reassuring ritual, almost another annual observance: "as the season approached they would say: 'The time for the throwing of stones [at the sparrows that eat the grass shoots] has come'" (91). The ritual aspect is emphasized by the timing of this episode—immediately after the cherry-blossom excursion of chapter 19.

The symbolic significance of the garden is further suggested by its changelessness. Though its blossoms come and go with the seasons, the garden is unaffected by the flood, an exceptional event outside the normal cycle of nature. We have already seen that the garden shows no trace of the high waters when Sachiko goes to it after the flood. Yukiko, too, heads for the garden when she returns to Ashiya from Tokyo, right after the flood:

> Yukiko stopped O-haru, who was already on her way to the Stolz house [to call Sachiko]—they could hear children's voices in the garden—and went out to sit in a birch chair under the terrace awning.
>
> From the cab window, the damage around Narihira Bridge had

> seemed worse than she expected, but here everything was as it had always been. Not a leaf was disturbed. In the evening calm, hardly a breath of air touched the garden. The heat was intense, and the quiet gave the light and dark greens of the foliage a special limpidity. The green of the lawn seemed to rise up and flow through her.
>
> (201)

"Everything was as it had always been." This time the garden stands in contrast even to the rest of Ashiya: "The pines along the embankment were buried under a solid layer of dust. Unfortunately the blazing hot weather continued day after day and the cloud of dust only became more suffocating. There was little this year to bespeak the elegant suburb of Ashiya" (200). In the garden, though, "not a leaf was disturbed."

Such a garden is impossible if the description is read literally. If it is seen instead as a microcosm of an ideal world, a paradise that knows no time but the eternal cycle of the seasons, then the Ashiya garden falls into place alongside several other Tanizaki gardens. A garden that took on special meaning for the author is described in his *Childhood Years:*

> In Negishi there was a restaurant called the Okano, which had a splendid garden. I remember going there two or three times—perhaps after viewing the chrysanthemum displays at Dangozaka, in which case Mother may very well have been with us. The Okano had originally specialized in sweet bean soup, though other foods were also available. The rooms were large, designed to accommodate many parties of customers; and the Konohana garden, as it was called, was wonderful, with landscaped hills and pools fed by waterfalls, with springs and artfully placed stones and rocks. I felt as if I had been drawn into a dream world, a nobleman's private garden of the sort I had seen only on the stage and in historical prints.[19]

All the elements here suggest a paradise essentially like the Ashiya garden: a connection with ritualized, annual observances is established with the mention of the chrysanthemum festival; Mother is present; delicious food is served; nature, represented by rocks, water, and hills, is in harmony; and all is viewed through the eyes of a child who sees the garden as a "dream world."

Even Terukatsu, Lord of Musashi, who as a child is very grown-up, acts like a child when he goes into the garden with his wife:

> "Shall we hunt fireflies? Out in the garden?"
>
> Her lovely, bright eyes filled with the sudden joy that comes to a child who has just thought of something wonderful. Her plump cheeks glowed. . . .
>
> Taking the ladies-in-waiting with them, the young couple eagerly chased fireflies about the garden. . . .
>
> "I've already caught ten," Terukatsu cried out wildly.
>
> "Oh! I only have five!"
>
> "There's one, there's one—I'm going to get him!" She was right behind Terukatsu as he darted off in pursuit. Running around the pond and along the stream, competing for the same firefly, they looked more like a brother and sister at play than newlyweds.[20]

Terukatsu's childlike behavior lasts only as long as he is in the garden. Back inside, he reverts to his characteristic grim sadism.

The timeless garden where the eternal child seeks refuge from the quotidian world reaches its fullest development in *The Bridge of Dreams,* the focus of Chapter Eight. Naomi's garden is a different story. It is in front of the house, in full view of anyone passing by on the street, and in it Naomi cultivates emphatically foreign flowers, "zinnia, phlox and canna blossoms."[21] Jōji has already told us that "she loved Western flowers and knew the names—troublesome English names—of many flowers that I was unfamiliar with,"[22] and her favorite is the least Japanese of all flowers, the tulip. Naomi's garden represents dangerous aspirations, a rejection of the Japanese environment, and an infatuation with the West. Like the Ashiya garden, it helps to satisfy a longing; but where Naomi longs to be Western, the Makiokas long for harmony and repose.

Beyond the garden, the Kansai region (that which centers on Kyoto, Osaka, and Kobe) is idealized, especially in relation to Tokyo. The Japan of *The Makioka Sisters* is not representative of the ultra-nationalistic Japan of the late 1930s, despite references to current events. In one of the most influential essays on *The Makioka Sisters,* the critic Nakamura Shin'ichirō writes, "[T]he author has, as much as possible, distanced the life of the novel from the trends of history. The distance between Tokyo and Osaka is, in this novel, made far greater than it really is. The author has exerted all his efforts to purify, as much as possible, the place he chose for his escape from reality. If we emphasize this point, then we can say that *The Makioka Sisters* is less a novel of urban life than a fantasy-novel about an ideal society."[23] The world of *The Makioka Sisters* is, in Nakamura's words, an "alternative Japan": the Japan of middle-class Kansai, heir to the court culture of Kyoto and the merchant culture of Osaka, indeed, the heartland of Japanese civilization. Viewed from this perspective (which is the Makiokas' perspective), Tokyo—formerly the shogun's capital in the eastern hinterlands, and in the late 1930s the seat of a militaristic government and symbol of the "new Japan"—is "a distant, utterly foreign country" (217).[24] In this view, Kansai is the true Japan, the Japan of merchants, craftsmen, and courtiers; Tokyo is an aberration. Instead of parodying the military mystique as *The Secret History of the Lord of Musashi* does, *The Makioka Sisters* repudiates it by consigning it to Tokyo and minimizing its role in the Makiokas' world. Thus *The Makioka Sisters* is not "an escape from reality" but, in the context of the early 1940s, a subversive reminder of the non-military roots of Japanese culture, a lament for the decline of the Osaka merchant's way of life, and a sort of "secret history" of Japan from 1936 to 1941, narrating the reality that was missing from the "official histories" written in Tokyo.

Cosmopolitanism is an important aspect of the alternative Japan. Germans and Russians are depicted as real people, not as the stereotypes so often found in Japanese portrayals of Westerners, such as Madame Shlemskaya, the Russian dance teacher in *Naomi.* When Mrs. Stolz imagines the worst about her family during the flood, Sachiko, "looking into that tearful face, . . . could not think of the German woman as a foreigner," despite the language barrier between them (183). Japanese and German children play together; the Makiokas exchange gifts with the Germans, dine and gossip with the Russians. Even Yukiko is cosmopolitan: "People who did not know her well took Yukiko for a thoroughly Japanese lady, but only because the surface (the dress and appearance, speech and deportment) was so Japanese. The real Yukiko was quite different. She was even then studying French, and she understood Western music far better than Japanese" (19). It is not surprising that Yukiko is welcomed with cheese and her favorite white wine when she comes back from an unhappy visit to Tokyo (128–129).

Another feature of the idealized Kansai is that the Makiokas live in harmony with nature when they are at home. Yoshida Seiichi sees in both *The Makioka Sisters* and the *Genji* "a subtle weaving together of nature with daily life, of the seasons with emotions and the senses."[25] He offers this passage as an example of the traditional awareness of nature in a modern setting:

> In Ashiya too the coolness of autumn had come overnight. Sachiko and Teinosuke were facing each other across the breakfast table, . . . and it came to Sachiko . . . that the coffee in the kitchen smelled better than usual.
>
> "It is autumn," she remarked, glancing up from the paper. "Does it seem to you that the coffee smells stronger this morning?"
>
> (111)

Other examples are not difficult to find. As the family walks home from dinner with the Kyrilenkos, Sachiko says "What a nice smell. The cloves are in bloom somewhere." "Only one more month to the cherry blossoms," Taeko replies (80). Again, in late summer, Sachiko, just back from Tokyo, gazes at the Ashiya garden: "The garden carried just a suggestion of coolness, the smell of a sweet olive reminded her that in Ashiya too autumn was near. They would soon have to take in the reed awning" (243). Even in a tense moment, when Yukiko confronts Taeko with evidence of her misbehavior, nature is not forgotten: "Yukiko was toying with the chrysanthemum in the glass vase. Though she avoided her sister's eye, her voice was calm, her hand steady, and she showed no sign of excitement" (469).

Tokyo is a different story. Dusty and windy, always either too cold or too hot, the capital is at odds with nature whenever the Makiokas go there:

> Magnificent though the Ginza might be, there was something dry and harsh in the air that made [Sachiko] sure she would always be a stranger there. . . . As the cab approached Shibuya, she felt somehow chilly even in the summer night. . . . The shops were imposing and there was considerable evidence of prosperity as they started up the hill beyond Shibuya. Why then was it so lacking in warmth; why were the faces so cold and white? Sachiko thought of her own Ashiya, and of Kyoto. If this were Kyoto, she could feel at home in a street she was seeing for the first time.
>
> (217)

Tsuruko's Shibuya house—new and superficially attractive, but cramped, drafty, and unstable—is an appropriate emblem of the Tokyo of the novel.

The preeminent symbol of natural beauty in *The Makioka Sisters* is the most Japanese of flowers, the cherry. In Japanese court poetry, the conventional response to falling cherry blossoms is one of appreciation mingled with anxiety and regret over the passing of beauty and time, with an analogy being drawn between the fate of the blossoms and human existence. These examples are from the *Kokinshū:*

> Yo no naka ni taete sakura no nakariseba
> haru no kokoro wa nodokekaramashi
>
> If in this world there were no cherry blossoms—none at all—
> Then the soul of spring might have been serene.
>
> (no. 53, by Ariwara no Narihira)

The response also includes a sad resignation to the inevitable:

> Chiru hana o nani ka uramin
> yo no naka ni waga mi mo tomo ni aran mono ka wa
>
> I shall not lament the scattering cherry blossoms—in this world
> is there any chance at all that I might linger with them?
>
> (no. 112, anonymous)

The controlling image of *The Makioka Sisters,* given in the title *Sasameyuki,* suggests that the Makiokas' idealized Kansai is a world on the brink—a forest of cherries still in bloom but already beginning to flutter gently to the ground like snow. Though the Makiokas turn to their garden for solace, they know that the blossoms will fall, that Yukiko will marry, and that the world will change. Their response is the traditional one of gratitude for the moment of beauty, anxiety, regret, and resignation, all felt simultaneously; and such, too, is likely to be the reader's response to the novel. The reader can also share feelings of gratitude that "at least this much was written down,"[26] because a desire to preserve the beautiful moment, whether in a photograph, a poem, or a novel, is another inevitable response. For example:

Mume ga ka o sode ni utsushite todometeba
haru wa sugu tomo katami naramashi

Let me imbue my sleeve with the fragrance of the plum blossoms—
The spring will pass away but I will have a keepsake.

(*Kokinshū* no. 46, anonymous)

Oshi to omou kokoro wa ito ni yorarenan
chiru hana goto ni nukite todomen

Would that I could twist my grieving heart into a thread—
Then I would catch the falling blossoms one by one and fix them here to stay.

(*Kokinshū* no. 114, by Sosei)

Teinosuke's poem at the end of chapter 19—at the conclusion of the definitive cherry excursion—is in the same tradition:

Ito semete hanamigoromo ni hanabira o
himete okamashi haru no nagori ni[27]

Let me hide at least a petal
In the sleeve of my flower-viewing robe,
That I may remember the spring.

(91)

We cannot stop time, but we can cherish our secret memories.

SEVEN

Captain Shigemoto's Mother

Japan in the late 1940s was picking up the pieces, groping for a new identity under a foreign occupation, the nation's self-confidence shaken and its military tradition discredited. The Korean War, which helped to spark Japan's economic recovery, was in the future. Food was still being rationed; black markets were thriving. It was in these years of deprivation that Tanizaki emerged as the preeminent figure in Japanese letters with the complete publication of *The Makioka Sisters*, his receipt of the Order of Culture from the emperor in November, 1949, and the publication in 1949–1950 of *Captain Shigemoto's Mother*—his first piece of fiction after *The Makioka Sisters.* "This may be Mr. Tanizaki's greatest masterpiece," wrote Masamune Hakuchō. "*Shigemoto's Mother* makes it clearer than ever that Mr. Tanizaki is a consummate writer."[1] The critic Kamei Katsuichirō wrote that *Shigemoto's Mother* "encompasses all the elements of Tanizaki's writing, it is their ultimate crystallization."[2]

Captain Shigemoto's Mother was the last novel Tanizaki wrote for newspaper serialization. He began negotiations with the Osaka *Mainichi Shimbun* after he had completed *The Makioka Sisters* in May 1948. At first he planned to serialize the sequel to *The Secret History of the Lord of Musashi,* postponed since 1933, but instead he decided on a novel set in the Heian court of the tenth century.[3] He began writing *Shigemoto's Mother* as soon as he completed his move to an estate near the Shimogamo Shrine in Kyoto in April 1949, and completed it before serialization began in November. This was a remarkably short time for Tanizaki, who often lamented that he could write no more than two or three pages a day.

Tanizaki's interest in the Heian period was nothing new. His first published work, the play *Tanjō* (Birth, 1910), is based on eleventh-century sources and set in the Heian court, and a number of stories and plays that he wrote between 1911 and 1918 have Heian settings.[4] Reminders of Heian culture also figure in several works from the early 1930s—*Arrowroot, The Secret History of the Lord of Musashi,* and *The Reed Cutter.* It was probably around this time that the idea for *Shigemoto's Mother* began to germinate. One of Tanizaki's principal sources for *Shigemoto* was discovered in 1931—*Heichū monogatari,* also known as *Heichū nikki* (Tales of Heichū, Diary of Heichū), a tenth-century work similar to other *uta nikki* or *uta monogatari* (poem-diaries or poem-tales) such as *Ise monogatari* and *Yamato monogatari* (Tales of Ise, Tales of Yamato).[5] It was also around this time that Tanizaki told Satō Haruo he wanted to write a novel in the form of an *uta nikki.*[6] In 1935 he began his first modern-Japanese translation of *The Tale of Genji,* which was followed by *The Makioka Sisters,* with its many reminders of court culture. Just before *Shigemoto's Mother* he published "Fujitsubo," a translation of passages he had omitted from his first *Genji;* and right after completing *Shigemoto's Mother* he began his second *Genji* translation.[7]

Before *Shigemoto's Mother,* Tanizaki had already offered imaginative, alternative "histories" in *Arrowroot, A Tale of Chrysanthemums in Chaos, A Blind Man's Tale, The Secret History of the Lord of Musashi, A Portrait of Shunkin, Kikigakishō,* and *The Makioka Sisters.* Each but the last of these takes the form of an historical novel, but, as Tanizaki admitted, they are largely the products of his imagination (19:418). The relationship of his material to actual events varies in these works, one extreme being represented by *A Blind Man's Tale,* an imaginative elaboration on people and events that every Japanese pupil would have been familiar with, and the other extreme by *The Secret History of the Lord of Musashi,* which is pure fabrication. Tanizaki points out in his introduction to *Chrysanthemums in Chaos* that the tale takes place in the late fifteenth and early sixteenth centuries, a period that few people know anything about. "The author set his eye on this era," he writes, "not because he wanted to uncover unknown historical facts or characters, but because the age leaves free room for his imagination."[8] "Tokugawa *gesaku* writers made Koremori the adopted son of a sushi-shop keeper," he continues. "I doubt that I will be able to muster that kind of audacity, but I hope that I can be uninhibited, even if it means that historians will scold me a little" (23:130).

Captain Shigemoto's Mother differs from earlier Tanizaki works in its relationship to the historical background. "While striving to be faithful to historical facts," Tanizaki admitted, "I seek out the gaps in the historical record and there unfold my own world" (23:234); but he does not identify the "gaps" in the story of Shigemoto's mother, and his "own world" is so skillfully woven into the historical fabric that most readers will cross the line between documented and imaginative history without realizing that a line exists. In his preface to the 1951 edition of *Shigemoto's Mother,* Tanizaki explains, "For the most part this work is derived from classics of the Heian period. The author has named each of them and made it clear which sections are drawn from these sources. . . . The name of one fictional document—a 'source' fabricated by the author—is also included, however, and the passages relating to it are products of the author's imagination. This is already clear to those who know the name of the document, and the question has nothing to do with the literary value of this work. In consideration of the general reader's interest, therefore, the author has chosen not to identify the fictional source here" (23:248–249).

All of the major characters—Shigemoto's mother (the central figure) and the men in orbit around her (her lover Heijū, her first husband Kunitsune, her second husband Shihei, her sons Shigemoto and Atsutada)—appear in authentic Heian texts, which are cited in the novel; but one of the "sources," *Shigemoto no nikki* (Shigemoto's Diary), is indeed fabricated.[9] Most developments in the last four chapters of the novel—Shigemoto's encounters with his father Kunitsune and the reunion with his mother—are "based" on Shigemoto's diary and so are of Tanizaki's invention, while the events of the earlier chapters follow classical sources more or less faithfully. Heijū's theft of Jijū's toilet box, for example, is adapted closely from *Konjaku monogatarishū* (Tales of Times Now Past; twelfth century).[10]

The fictitious *Shigemoto's Diary* is slipped in among authentic sources so that the transition is natural and plausible. The summary in chapter 7 of the fate of Shihei and his progeny concludes with a discussion of Atsutada, Shihei's son by Shigemoto's mother; and chapter 8, logically enough, proposes to tell what became of Kunitsune and *his* progeny. At the end of chapter 7, the personality and love affairs of Shigemoto's half-brother Atsutada are described and a number of his poems are quoted; the discussion of Atsutada refers to no fewer than six classical sources and quotes six poems from Heian collections. This much attention might be excessive, since Atsutada himself never appears in the novel, but a great deal more is known about him than about Shigemoto—Atsutada serves as a relatively solid foundation upon which to fabricate Shigemoto. More important, the authentic classical citations at the end of chapter 7 prepare the reader for the introduction of *Shigemoto's Diary* in chapter 8. As chapter 7 ends with examples of Atsutada's poetry, chapter 8 begins with several of Shigemoto's, gleaned from *Tales of Yamato* and the *Gosenshū* (Later Selection of Poetry), both from the tenth century. "These references are commonly known," says the narrator, "but there is another, which is not so widely read, a manuscript in the collection of the Shūkokaku Library called *Shigemoto's Diary*" (136).[11] It hardly occurs to the reader to question the authenticity of this new source, when the narrator cites more than thirty authentic sources. The subsequent paraphrases of *Shigemoto's Diary* seem plausible precisely because earlier paraphrases of authentic sources are accurate, and because *Shigemoto's Diary* is presented in the same learned style. The reader is further beguiled by the fact that the first episode based on *Shigemoto's Diary*, in which Heijū writes a poem on Shigemoto's arm, can be partially verified in authentic sources. The episode has already been mentioned briefly in chapter 6, where the source of the story (the headnote to *Gosenshū* no. 711) is quoted, and its reappearance in the context of *Shigemoto's Diary* helps prepare the reader to accept the purely fictional material that follows.

In fact, the headnote says simply "a child of the lady's"; the novel specifies that the child was Shigemoto. There is a good deal of fiction even in the first seven chapters of *Shigemoto's Mother*, the chapters based on authentic sources. Passages that appear to be straight exposition often embellish upon, or even deviate from, the sources. There is no evidence, for example, that either Shigemoto or his mother was still alive in 944, the year they are reunited in the novel. One fairly reliable source has Shigemoto dying in 931.[12] In the world of the novel, however, Shigemoto cannot meet his mother until his half-brother Atsutada is dead. Atsutada is known to have died in 943, and so Shigemoto and his mother must be kept alive at least that long.[13]

The clearest example of Tanizaki's adapting the historical past to his fictional world is Kunitsune's surrender of his wife to Shihei. Kunitsune—old, impotent, and therefore, he believes, unable to make his young wife happy—feels guilty for monopolizing her and yields her to his nephew Shihei. The episode is adapted from an account in *Tales of Times Now Past*,[14] but in Tanizaki's hands it becomes another manifestation of the common Tanizaki motif in which a man yields a woman to a younger man. Often the man is unable to satisfy the woman sexually; the woman is usually, but not always, his wife. Citing a passage in Tanizaki Matsuko's memoirs, some commentators have assumed that the theme originated in Tanizaki's feelings for her,[15] but it appears in his work as early as the 1914 novella *Jōtarō*. Jōtarō, the title character, takes his former student and rival Shōji to see Otama, the woman they both love. Simultaneously attracted to both Shōji and Otama, Jōtarō grovels before them: "Many times he had tried to love this boy with the same passion as he would a woman and always failed. But now he became aware of an indescribable feeling of love and worship gradually overcoming the anger within him. The more strength and arrogance the youth [Shōji] displayed the greater was Jōtarō's masochistic feeling of joy in being overcome."[16]

In this motif, then, the older man typically allows himself to be "overcome"—succeeded, superseded—by a younger man (or, in *Manji* [Quicksand, 1928–1930], by a woman) with whom he identifies and to whom he may be attracted. There is a wide range of examples. Kaname (in *Tade kuu mushi* [Some Prefer Nettles, 1928–1929]), having lost interest in his wife sexually, encourages her to have an affair. In *Quicksand*, Kakiuchi condones his wife's lesbian relationship with Mitsuko, to whom he, too, is attracted. Seribashi (in *The Reed Cutter*) teaches his son to love Oyū as he has loved her. The ailing professor in *Kagi* (The Key, 1956), believing that he is inadequate to his wife's sexual demands, encourages her relationship with the handsome young Kimura, both to assuage his sense of guilt and to enflame his jealousy and sex drive; and his wife, addressing her husband through her diary, observes that "[Kimura] is identified with you, you are part of him, the two of you are really one."[17] The dying father in *The Bridge of Dreams* passes the baton, both psychological and carnal, to his son. Finally, the impotent old man of *Fūten rōjin nikki* (Diary of a Mad Old Man, 1961–1962) pushes his daughter-in-law, to whom he is powerfully attracted, into an affair with his nephew. The old man is explicit about the process by which he derives vicarious enjoyment: "I can be near a beautiful woman without arousing suspicion. And to make up for my own inability, I can get her involved with a handsome man, plunge the whole household into turmoil, and take pleasure in *that*. . . . Now that I can't enjoy the thrill myself any more, I can at least have the pleasure of watching someone else risk a love affair."[18] In *Shigemoto's Mother*, Tanizaki shapes the episode from *Tales of Times Now Past* to fit the pattern of an older man yielding his wife to a younger, and Shihei becomes the first of Kunitsune's alter egos.

Judiciously chosen images accentuate the relationship between Kunitsune and his other alter ego, Shigemoto. The novel describes two memorable encounters between father and son. The first is set in Kunitsune's garden, where the old man teaches his son to recite verses by Po Chü-i that express his longing, and the second, at a riverbed burial ground where Kunitsune practices the Contemplation of Impurity in an attempt to forget his wife. Kunitsune's preoccupations, Chinese poetry and Buddhism, are foreign and conventionally masculine. Both encounters between father and son take place in autumn, the season of melancholy, decline, and impending death. The sensory imagery associated with Kunitsune is cold, harsh, and colorless: the morning after giving away his wife, he wakes up cold; Shigemoto is chilled by the cold ground under his feet and by the dew on his collar as he follows his father to the burial ground; and the cold, white moonlight that ruthlessly illuminates the corpses looks like frost on the ground—a simile that recalls a well-known verse by Li Po:

> The moon shines brightly before my bed—
> I took it for frost on the ground.

Raising my head I gaze at the moon;
Bowing my head I think of my home.[19]

The imagery reinforces the foreign associations that have already been established for Kunitsune. References to Buddhist treatises and *setsuwa* collections give the passage a cerebral quality that is in keeping with Kunitsune and his attempts to escape his grief and so contributes to the effect of the image cluster.

The old man reminds one of the priest in Ueda Akinari's *The Blue Hood*, who goes mad with grief and devours the corpse of a beloved acolyte, then tries to free himself from his obsession by meditating on a couplet from a T'ang religious poem.[20] Kunitsune emerges from the burial ground a complex figure: grotesque yet appealing; cerebral yet emotional; distant, but sympathetic because he is so humanly weak. Through the imagery deployed around him, he is relentlessly associated with harsh light, foreign poetry and religion, cold, decline, decay, and death.

Kunitsune's Buddhist practices offer Shigemoto one way to overcome the loss of his mother. The imagery, as Shigemoto follows his father under the clear, cold moon, their shadows sharp against the white ground, echoes imagery in "Longing for Mother," *The Secret History of the Lord of Musashi*, and *The Reed Cutter*. In a dream, the narrator of "Longing for Mother" searches for his mother through just such a moonlit landscape. As a boy, the man in the reeds in *The Reed Cutter* has followed his father on long walks in the moonlight to Oyū's villa, where they peer at her through a hedge. Hōshimaru, in *The Secret History*, twice moves furtively through bright moonlight: first, when he follows an old woman on a cold, winter night to the storehouse where he sees the scene that will dominate his fantasy life; and second, when he slips out of the castle a few nights later to try to enact his fantasy for the first time: "It was about two o'clock in the morning when the boy started down the path. The moon that had cast its pale glow on his nightly visits to the attic rested now on the ridge of Mount Ojika and inscribed his shadow sharply on the ground. He held a thin veil over his head so that he would look like a woman fleeing the castle; as he walked he saw its tremulous shadow float across the ground like a jellyfish."[21] The imagery in the burial-ground scene suggests that Shigemoto, like these other characters, is approaching a liminal experience, perhaps the catalyst for an obsession. Crossing a bridge over a stream (an image repeated in *The Bridge of Dreams*) on the way to the burial ground, Kunitsune and Shigemoto enter a world apart, and "[t]he sight of his father kneeling like a solitary shadow in these surroundings made Shigemoto feel that he had been drawn into a weird dream world" (156–157). Shigemoto seems to be on the brink of discovering "in the innermost recesses of his heart," as Hōshimaru does, "a deep well of a different constitution, beyond the reach of his self-discipline."[22] In a different novel, Shigemoto might have become a necrophiliac. But the dream that Kunitsune offers is the wrong dream at the wrong time—Shigemoto "was summoned back willy-nilly to the world of reality by the putrid smell that assaulted his nostrils" (157). As he listens to his father's explanation of the Contemplation of Impurity, Shigemoto wants to cry out, "Father, please don't make Mother into something dirty" (166). Hōshimaru goes back to the storehouse night after night, but one such night is enough for Shigemoto; he never accompanies his father to the burial mounds again.

Shigemoto's reunion with his mother in the next chapter contrasts sharply with the burial-ground scene. The latter has an intellectual tone, but the reunion is lyrical and, though the story originates with Tanizaki, almost every detail has precedents in Heian literature. The setting, at the western foot of Mount Hiei, is rich in literary associations. The full moon softened by the spring mist is the *oborozuki* of Heian poetry and of the *Genji*, not the ominous, cold moon of Kunitsune's autumn. It shines warmly on cherry blossoms and on the *yamabuki*, two of the favorite flowers of court poets, and under the cherry tree stands a nun veiled in white. The result is to associate Shigemoto's mother with the familiar and the traditional—native poetry; spring haze; cherry blossoms; the lingering fragrance of incense; soft, reassuring shadows; and the promise of life held by spring and by motherhood.

The image of a beautiful woman under a tree echoes countless Japanese works from ancient times to *The Makioka Sisters*. The familiar poem by Ōtomo no Yakamochi (718–785) is an early example:

Haru no sono kurenai niou
momo no hana shitateru michi ni idetatsu otome

A garden in spring–blossoming in fragrant pink
The flowers of the peach color the path beneath them where now steps forth a maiden.

(*Man'yōshū* XIX:4,139)

Tanizaki's fiction routinely associates cherry blossoms with motherhood and continuity. The narrator of *Arrowroot,* for example, recalls his mother showing him the blossoms at Yoshino, and the Makiokas' annual visits to the blossoms at the Heian Shrine reinforce their ties with the past and give order to their lives. The close association of the cherry tree with Shigemoto's mother is unmistakable. When Shigemoto sees her from a distance, standing in the moonlight under the blossoms, he mistakes her at first for a drooping, flower-laden branch. When he realizes that the figure is human, he imagines that she is the fairy of the uncannily beautiful tree. His mother does not simply appear: she emerges from the blossoms as though created from them by some wonderful alchemy.

The image of a woman under a tree has Buddhist associations as well, because of the tradition that Maya gave birth to Siddhartha under a tree, and so is doubly appropriate for Shigemoto's mother, who has become a Buddhist nun. The theme of Buddhism is common to both the burial-ground scene and the reunion; but Kunitsune's Buddhism is ascetic, harsh, and cerebral, while Shigemoto's mother's is a gentler, more compassionate, more domesticated–in a word, more maternal–form. The full moon, a common symbol of Buddhist enlightenment, is a spring moon here; the full moons of "Longing for Mother," *The Secret History, The Reed Cutter,* and the burial ground are autumnal. Even her incense has both Buddhist and secular, even romantic, connotations. A famous love poem, already cited in connection with *Arrowroot,* comes to mind when Mother's incense reminds Shigemoto of the past.

Satsuki matsu hanatachibana no ka o kageba
mukashi no hito no sode no ka zo suru

The orange blossoms that wait for early summer
Bear the fragrance of the sleeves of the one of old.

(*Kokinshū* no. 139, anonymous)

The narrative gradually prepares the reader to accept Shigemoto's mother as an ideal figure capable of embodying both the maternal and the Buddhist. Her full name is never given; she is always "principal wife" (*kita no kata*), "the Ariwara lady," "Shigemoto's mother," or simply "mother." Her face is described as "mysterious," "beautiful," and "small," but individual traits are omitted. Shigemoto cannot see her face clearly when he visits her as a young child, and she is already described in transcendent terms—"It was like peering reverently at an image of the Buddha ensconced deep in a shrine, and he never had a full, satisfying look" (139). She takes no action and rarely speaks.

Classical sources, however, reveal more about the lady and her family than the novel does. The narrator provides detailed information on her son Atsutada, but neglects to say that her brother Motokata was (like Atsutada) one of the Thirty-six Sages of Poetry, and that her elder sister is mentioned in *Tales of Yamato* and *Gosenshū*.[23] The narrator also suppresses a report that Shigemoto's mother was "flirtatious, and she was not at all pleased at finding herself married to an elderly husband."[24]

The idealization of Shigemoto's mother is enhanced by the points of view from which she is described—those of the men who love her and who are least likely to be objective. When Kunitsune peers at her, wondering what feelings lie hidden in her heart, he finds her face "mysterious" and "enigmatic" (88). To the child Shigemoto, she is at first a sweet fragrance, then a beautiful face wreathed in soft spring light. After their separation, Shigemoto believes that she is too remote for him to approach—almost a being of another world. When he finally does meet her after forty years and looks up at her face, it is "blurred by the light of the moon filtering through the cherry blossoms; sweet and small, *it looked as though it were framed by a halo*" (179; emphasis added). The events of the last four chapters, based on *Shigemoto's Diary*, are seen through a child's eyes, and the most memorable pictures of both Kunitsune and his wife are sketched by Shigemoto from his childhood memories. A child's eye being an effective filter on events, all but a few essential details are blurred, while those that are remembered are endowed with the mystery, the beauty, or the horror most likely to impress a child. Shigemoto's fragmentary childhood memories are, in turn, filtered through the intelligence of the narrator, who selects and interprets. To Kunitsune and Shigemoto, then, Shigemoto's mother is not an individual woman with distinctive traits, but an idealization of womanhood and motherhood.

In their longing for Shigemoto's mother, father and son are one. The same trio—a dead or dying father, a beloved wife-mother, and a young son who eagerly assumes his father's role in adoring her—appears in *The Reed Cutter* and *The Bridge of Dreams* as well. On the one hand, Kunitsune has qualities of a child—"the eighty-year-old Major Counselor wanted to wail, like a child calling for his mother" when he realizes that his wife is gone (111); and he is scolded like a child by Shigemoto's nurse (150–151). On the other hand, Shigemoto is Kunitsune's emotional heir. He perpetuates his father's longing for many years after his father's death, and when he is reunited with his mother at the end of the novel, he is both his mother's son and his father's surrogate. This is one reason the reunion scene is so powerful.

In longing for Mother, then, Shigemoto is Kunitsune's alter ego, but father and son respond differently to the lady's departure. Kunitsune turns to drink, Chinese poetry, and Buddhist sūtras to help him forget his wife, and tries to neutralize and purge his love by forcing himself to think of her as a decomposing corpse, but his attempts to forget her—or to turn her into something dirty, as Shigemoto puts it—fail. Shigemoto idealizes his mother and thereby avoids his father's misery:

> "Mother," to him, was nothing more than the memory of a tearful face that he had glimpsed in his fifth year and the sensory awareness of her fragrant incense. For forty years, memory and awareness were cherished, gradually beautified into an ideal, and purified, until they had become something vastly different from the reality.
>
> (144)

Even after all obstacles have disappeared, Shigemoto lets years go by before he visits her, because he prefers his beautiful memories:

> It seems likely that Shigemoto wanted to go on forever adoring his mother just as he had seen her in his childhood. He had been angry with his father, deploring the desecration of his mother's image when the old Counselor practiced the Contemplation of Impurity, and during forty years of separation he had cherished an idealized version of his mother, which he had constructed from the image that lingered vaguely in his memory. What would she look like now, forty years later, having left the world after so many changes and become a servant of the Buddha? The mother Shigemoto remembered was an aristocratic woman of twenty or twenty-one, with long hair and full cheeks, but his mother the nun, living alone in a hut at Nishi-Sakamoto, was an old woman past sixty years of age. The thought must naturally have caused Shigemoto to shrink from facing cold reality. It may have seemed far better to embrace forever the image of the past, savoring his memories of her gentle voice, the sweet fragrance of her incense, and the sensation of her brush caressing his arm, rather than to drink rashly from the cup of disillusionment.
>
> (172)

Shigemoto's approach is the opposite of the holy men so skilled in the Contemplation of Impurity that "a living beauty will come to look revolting, not only in the subjective view of the ascetic himself but in the eyes of onlookers as well" (164); instead, Shigemoto's imagination turns an elderly nun into a beautiful young woman. Like Sasuke (in *A Portrait of Shunkin*), he is able to render time and age irrelevant: he clings to an idealization of his mother, rather than trying to "erase her lovely image from the depths of his heart" (165), as his father does, or seeking to interact with the woman herself. He admires Atsutada fondly from a distance because his half-brother resembles their mother. Even when Shigemoto finally does meet his mother again, he sees not the face of an old woman who has taken the tonsure, but a face "blurred by the light of the moon filtering through the cherry blossoms" that looks "as though it were framed by a halo," and so he is able to maintain his idealized image. Shigemoto himself ceases to be a middle-aged man: "in an instant he felt as though he had become a child of five or six," and "like a child secure in his mother's love, he wiped his tears again and again with her sleeve." Shigemoto's solution is far more gentle than Sasuke's, but finally he is like Sasuke in preferring a private, idealized version in place of the woman herself.

The apotheosis of Shigemoto's mother has precedents in Tanizaki's work but is nevertheless unusually explicit and complete. Shunkin is likened to "the Buddha Amida, coming to lead a devout believer to the Pure Land,"[25] but Shigemoto's mother actually becomes a religious figure. When Shigemoto asks her if she is the mother of the late Middle Counselor (Atsutada), she replies, "I was as you say, before I left the world [i.e., before taking Buddhist vows]" (179). Having "left the family" (*shukke*), in the standard Japanese expression, and become a nun, she is no longer Atsutada's or Shigemoto's mother. She has become even more than a nun. An ethereal, indistinct figure illuminated by the full moon and standing under a blossoming cherry tree, she represents the simultaneous realization of Eternal Mother and of Buddhist enlightenment.

EIGHT

The Bridge of Dreams

When Tanizaki first translated *The Tale of Genji,* in the late 1930s, the temper of the times led him to omit all references to Genji's affair with his stepmother Fujitsubo, because the imperial succession is disrupted when their child becomes emperor. A desire to restore this crucial story line was one of the motivations for Tanizaki's second *Genji* translation. Suffering from dizziness caused by high blood pressure, he employed an amanuensis, a scholarly young Kyoto woman named Ibuki Kazuko. He completed the new translation in 1954, after five years of work interrupted by poor health. He published *Yōshō jidai* (Childhood Years) in 1955–1956 and *Kagi* (The Key) in 1956. Early in 1958 he began serializing a novel called *Zangyakuki* (An Account of Brutality), about a man who has been left impotent by the atomic bomb, but a stroke forced him to abandon the project.

He dictated all of these works except part of *The Key*. Accustomed to writing in solitude with no interruptions, he worried that his work had suffered and concealed his use of an amanuensis. Only after publishing *The Bridge of Dreams* in 1959 did he acknowledge that he was no longer writing with his own hand.[1]

Tanizaki wrote that he lay awake at night mulling over the story, so anxious was he about this "first" attempt to dictate a piece of fiction (19:439). He told visitors that the work was going badly and, after it was published, he wrote, "Though most readers might not notice, I'm sure that anyone who reads *The Bridge of Dreams* carefully will see that it's different from what I've written before" (21:501). His misgivings faded with time. When Ms. Ibuki asked him shortly before his death if he was unhappy with *The Bridge of Dreams*, he smiled and said, "No, I don't feel that way any more."[2] In 1964 he referred to the novella as a landmark in his career and expressed delight that it had been translated into English (19:439).

The Bridge of Dreams is the autobiography of Otokuni Tadasu, a man who longs for a tranquil, childhood world presided over by the Ideal Mother. As such, it has obvious affinities with *Haha o kouru ki* (Longing for Mother, 1919), *Arrowroot, The Reed Cutter,* and *Captain Shigemoto's Mother.* It has affinities with *A Portrait of Shunkin,* as well, though these are less obvious. Like Sasuke, Tadasu constructs, lives in, and strives to protect a fantasy world that he finds more appealing than mundane reality; and the narrative situation, as in *Shunkin,* reflects the ambiguity of his dream world.

In the broadest sense, Tadasu's world encompasses Kyoto, the city that more than any other represents Japanese continuity. Tadasu is a part of Kyoto. His family name is the name of a district in southwestern Kyoto; his given name is the name of the deity enshrined at Shimogamo, near Tadasu's home, and Tadasu Forest surrounds the shrine and Tadasu's estate. In another sense, however, Kyoto—even Tadasu Forest—is marginal to Tadasu's dream world. The center of his fantasy life is the estate he occupies with his parents, a traditional house facing south on a landscape garden. The estate is minutely described, down to the exact size and arrangement of the rooms and the disposition of plants, buildings and other features of the garden.[3]

The marvelous evocation of the setting in *The Bridge of Dreams* recalls similar effects in *Arrowroot* and *The Reed Cutter* but, being limited to Tadasu's estate, is focused on a tiny area. The city of Kyoto and the countryside beyond are scarcely evoked at all; they lie beyond the hazy illumination of Tadasu's fantasies. Outside the estate, only the remote village of Shizuichino is described in any detail, and Tadasu's dry account of it contrasts with his loving portrait of home. Shizuichino is part of the harsh, stressful, uncooperative world that lies outside Tadasu's dream world and that he prefers to avoid.

It is Tadasu's father who first treats the estate as a refuge, and his wife (Tadasu's mother) is a central figure in it:

> He put in an appearance at his bank now and then, but spent most of his time at home, seldom inviting guests. . . .
> All of my father's love was concentrated on my mother. With this house, this garden, and this wife, he seemed perfectly happy.
> (100)

The estate's detachment from the city reinforces the isolation of Tadasu's world. The site is in Tadasu Forest between the Takano River, to the east, and a shallow stream to the west, with the Shimogamo Shrine across the stream to the northwest. The stream, shrine, and forest themselves are suspended in time, relatively unaffected by the modern city that surrounds them on all sides. When Tadasu crosses the "narrow stone bridge" (97) to his estate, he steps even farther from the outside world into the world of his dreams. The Chinese couplet at the gate is an invitation to enter a carefree world apart:

> Deep in the grove the many birds are gay.
> Far from the dust the pine and bamboo are clean.
> (99)[4]

Tadasu's garden, the heart of his retreat, is even more important symbolically than the Makioka's garden at Ashiya. Like other paradise-gardens, it is a microcosm where father, mother, and child eat peacefully together among water, rocks, and flowers that represent the harmony of nature. A safe, isolated world, the garden is a place in which Tadasu can play freely, indulge his fantasies, even make love to his stepmother. On the far side of Tadasu's pond is a tea cottage, his favorite spot to play as a child. It is reached by crossing a second bridge, which leads him still deeper into the garden. People involved in the world of tea sometimes think of the tea cottage as a microcosm, even a womb, in part because of the humble dimensions and tiny doorways characteristic of these structures. Tadasu's cottage, too, where he entertains himself for hours playing with his grandfather's tea implements and watching centipedes, is a retreat, a womb within the larger paradise of the garden. Ultimately the garden—green, damp, warm, and growing—represents life. A useful contrast is the burial ground in *Captain Shigemoto's Mother,* dominated by cold, harsh, white images representing death.

Tadasu leaves the estate regularly to go to school or to work, but he barely mentions these outings. His body crosses the bridge to the outside world, but his heart stays at home. His only dependable link with society is his nurse, Okane. Since the unpleasant realities of the outside world have no place within the estate, she takes him for a walk through Tadasu Forest when she wants to give him news from outside. Even then, Tadasu fails or refuses to grasp the significance of what she tells him. Her revelations do not penetrate the haze of his dream world.

At the core of Tadasu's dream are the warmth and security of Mother's breast. As a small child, he falls asleep in his mother's arms:

> The mingled scents of her hair and milk hovered there in her bosom, around my face. As dark as it was, I could still dimly see her white breasts.
>
> . . . She would sing [her usual lullaby] over and over while I drifted off into a peaceful sleep, still clutching her breasts and running my tongue around her nipples. Gradually I would slip into the world of dreams.
>
> (106–107. Hibbett's translation omits the last sentence [18:157].)

After his mother's death, Tadasu longs for "[t]hat sweet, dimly white dream world there in her warm bosom" (109); and Okane comforts him by saying that, if he prays, his mother will come to see him in his dreams. When Tadasu's father remarries and Tadasu is allowed to sleep with his stepmother, "[t]hat warm, dimly white dream world—the world I thought had disappeared forever—had unexpectedly returned" (119). When he is nineteen years old, Tadasu relives it with his stepmother yet again: "The moment I saw her breasts there before me, so unexpectedly revealed, I was back in the dream world that I had longed for, back in the power of the memories that had haunted me for so many years" (134).

Tadasu's imagery associates his dream world with the gentle stability of the natural cycle. Like the idealized Kansai of *The Makioka Sisters,* his world is in harmony with nature. Events flow with the seasons and are dated by reference to flora. Tadasu's real mother dies, for example, "early one autumn, just as the chestnut tree at our doorway was beginning to shed its leaves" (107); and he first meets his stepmother-to-be "in the spring, when the double globeflowers at the mouth of the waterfall were in full bloom" (111–112).[5] Tadasu's world resembles the world of *The Tale of Genji* in this respect. As Edward Seidensticker had observed, "[I]t is not often through the whole enormous length of the work . . . that we are unaware of the season and the phase of the moon. . . . In the *Genji* the seasons float by and the characters float with them, in a single continuum."[6]

Events that interrupt Tadasu's dream and involve him with people on the outside are dated by the calendar, which is made to seem artificial, even clinical. An example is the chronology of his father's illness, which involves visits to and from the doctor and disrupts the tranquil routine:

> If it was last fall that Father became aware of his unhappy fate, he was then forty-three years old, Mother was thirty, and I was eighteen. (141)

> It was in August that Father lost the strength to get out of bed. (142)

> He lived about three more days, until the beginning of October. (147)

At such times, the nervous rationality of the calendar replaces the seasonal cycle that prevails when Tadasu's life is going smoothly. Nature is farthest out of balance shortly before Father's death: "It was one day in late September, the day after an unusually heavy rainstorm when the 'Shallow Stream' overflowed its banks and backed up into our pond, clouding the water, that Mother and I were summoned to Father's bedside" (143–144).

The most conspicuous image in the garden is the "water mortar," whose steady "clack, clack" is Tadasu's earliest memory of his estate. He often mentions it when he thinks of Mother. The rhythmic sound mingles with her voice as she sings a lullaby:

> Often my dreams were penetrated by the distant clack of the water mortar, far beyond my shuttered windows.
>
> Okane also knew a number of lullabies, . . . but I was never easily lulled asleep by her songs. (Nor, in the room I shared with her, could

> I hear the sound of the water mortar.) Mother's voice had a seductive rhythm all its own, a rhythm that filled my mind with pleasant fancies and quickly put me to sleep.
>
> (107)

Because of these memories, the sound of the mortar fills Tadasu with longing after his mother's death. When his father remarries and Tadasu nurses for the first time at his stepmother's breast, he "could hear the clack of the bamboo mortar. Everything was the way it used to be" (118).

The device is also associated with the paternal role in Tadasu's world. As long as Tadasu's father is healthy and functioning as head of the household, the mortar functions normally, too, even when Tadasu is between mothers; but when Tadasu nurses with his stepmother at the age of nineteen—in a sense usurping his father's role—he does not mention the mortar, even though it has been an integral part of his "white dream." The mortar is stopped when Father's health fails and he lies dying. After his death, Mother has the gardener start it up again to ease her loneliness.[7] In short, when life is stable, the steady flow of water through the clacking mortar parallels the natural flow of the seasons and accentuates the security and timelessness of Tadasu's world; but when that stability is disrupted, the flow is diverted, the mortar is silent, and artificial time asserts itself.

Much as Tadasu would like his world to be immutable, changes are of course inevitable. His mother dies, his relationship with his stepmother evolves, his father falls ill, Takeshi is born and sent away, Tadasu's father dies, Tadasu marries, and his stepmother dies. In *The Bridge of Dreams* Tadasu narrates his struggle to overcome these changes and maintain his dream world despite them. His narrative obscures some important details about the changes and about his countermeasures by withholding information and manipulating the chronology of events. "[A]ll that I record here is true," he asserts. "I do not allow myself the slightest falsehood or distortion. But there are limits even to telling the truth; there is a line one ought not to cross. And so, although I certainly never write anything untrue, neither do I write the whole of the truth. . . . If anyone says that not to tell the whole truth is in fact to lie, that is his own interpretation. I shall not venture to deny it" (140–141). The narrator of Tanizaki's "Watakushi" (The Thief, 1921) makes a similar declaration to his friends:

"Haven't I been telling you the truth over and over again? . . . But you didn't understand. . . . I've never lied to you, have I? You may ask why I didn't come out and tell you the whole truth. You probably think I was deceiving you after all. But try looking at it from my position. I'm sorry, but stealing is one thing I can't control." His next words state what Tadasu only implies: "Still, I don't like to deceive you, so *I told you the truth in a roundabout way.* I couldn't be any more honest than that—it's your fault for not taking my hints. Maybe you think I'm just being perverse, but I've never been more serious."[8]

This anticipates the challenge that Tanizaki poses at the end of his "Postscript" to *A Portrait of Shunkin:* "To the criticism that I have not written about the psychology of Shunkin and Sasuke, I should like to respond with a question: what need is there to describe their psychology? Is it not clear from what I have written?"[9] Tadasu, too, tells his story "in a roundabout way" and invites the reader to find "the whole of the truth" between the lines.

The first thing to do is to set the chronology straight. There is one major distortion: the onset of Father's illness precedes by many months Takeshi's birth and Tadasu's nursing at the age of nineteen, but Tadasu narrates the birth and nursing first. This distortion, the most significant chronological manipulation in the novella, obscures the possible cause-and-effect relationships among Father's illness, Takeshi's conception, and subsequent developments, which include Okane's decision to tell Tadasu about his stepmother, Takeshi's being sent away, and the changing relationship between Tadasu and his stepmother. Here is the true chronology:

1906:	Tadasu is born.
1911:	Tadasu's mother dies.
Spring, 1923:	Tadasu enters higher school, learns his stepmother's name.
August or September, 1924:	Takeshi is conceived.
Autumn, 1924:	Father sees Dr. Katō and learns of his illness.[10]
Late October, 1924:	Okane tells Tadasu about his stepmother's past.
January, 1925:	Tadasu learns that his stepmother is pregnant.

May, 1925:	Takeshi is born. In May or June, he is sent away, and Tadasu searches for him.
Mid June, 1925:	Tadasu nurses with his stepmother in the garden.
August, 1925:	Father is bedridden.
Late September, 1925:	Father gives his instructions to Tadasu.
Beginning of October, 1925:	Father dies.
November, 1926:	Tadasu marries Sawako.
June 27, 1928:	Tadasu's stepmother dies.
Spring, 1930:	Tadasu divorces Sawako.
1930:	Tadasu brings Takeshi to live with him.
June 27, 1931:	Tadasu completes *The Bridge of Dreams.*

The first major disruption in Tadasu's world is the death of his mother. Tadasu copes with this by identifying his stepmother with his mother. His confusion is possible because, instead of seeing them as individuals, he abstracts them into the Ideal Mother who presides over his dream world. The idealization begins even before his stepmother makes her first appearance. Tadasu scarcely recognizes his first mother in the photograph that his father has placed on the altar after her death. His father confirms that the photograph is "how she really looked at the time" (109), but Tadasu has constructed his own image of her, just as Sasuke creates an idealized image of Shunkin, and Shigemoto of his own mother. No photograph of the "real" woman could do justice to the image cherished by the man who idealizes her. When Tadasu says that he "felt an indescribable longing for my dead mother" (109), it is actually the "sweet, dimly white dream world" that he misses, because he conceives of his mother's death not as the death of an individual woman, but as the loss of his dream world: "Why wouldn't that world come back to me? Was Mother's death the death of that world? Where had she taken it?"[11]

Tadasu's stepmother can take the place of his mother not because she looks just like her, but because Tadasu and his father want her to fill the role. "To tell the truth," Tadasu admits, "if I'd been asked whether or not she looked like my mother I would scarcely have known what to say" (113). His father skillfully induces the boy to regard the new woman as an embodiment of his Ideal Mother, and not as a discreet individual. "When she comes you mustn't think of her as your second mother. Think that your mother has been away somewhere for a while and has just come home" (115). In retrospect, Tadasu recognizes his father's plan: "No doubt Father had instructed my present mother how to behave, and was trying his best to confuse me about what my two mothers had said or done, so that I would identify them in my mind. (117) . . . [I]t was his own extraordinary effort that enabled him to mold her in the image of my real mother" (124).

By the time he tells his story, however, Tadasu is accustomed to distinguishing his stepmother from his mother. He learns his stepmother's real name (Tsuneko) and begins to think of her as an individual in the spring of 1923. This is the next major change in his world: it is at this point that his relationship with her begins to change and sexual contact with her becomes possible. At the age of twelve or thirteen—in other words, at puberty—Tadasu has begun sleeping alone in his own room. Whenever he wants to sleep with his stepmother, she and his father permit it, but Tadasu obeys his father's orders—"Think of her as your real mother. You mustn't take the attitude that she's a stepmother" (120). This implies that the incest taboo prevents Tadasu from having intercourse with his stepmother as long as he confuses her with his real mother. The situation changes when he begins to think of her as Tsuneko, substitute mother and potential lover.

Takeshi is conceived seventeen or eighteen months later, in August or September, 1924. In the autumn of 1924, Tadasu's father learns of his illness, is warned to refrain from sexual intercourse, and has a premonition that he will die soon. By late October, he probably knows that his wife is pregnant, and it is then that Okane tells Tadasu about his stepmother's background. On reflection, Tadasu guesses that his father has orchestrated Okane's revelations: "'You mustn't let your father hear about it,' she had said, but might she not have done so on his instructions? Perhaps he had reason to want to sever the connection between my real mother and my stepmother, who had become so closely linked in my mind" (141). His stepmother reinforces the distinction as she encourages Tadasu (in June, 1925) to suckle at her breast: "'How is it? Does it remind you of how it used to taste? Your mother nursed you till you were four, I think.' It was extraordinary for my stepmother to say 'your mother' to me, distinguishing between herself and my father's first wife" (133). Tadasu sees his father's hand here, as well: "I hardly think Mother would have tried to tantalize me so shamelessly without his permission. . . . Possibly, knowing he hadn't long to live, he was trying to create a deeper intimacy between Mother and me, so that she would think of me as taking his place—and she made no objection" (141).[12]

"That is all I can bring myself to say," Tadasu writes at this point, having admitted that he has left part of his story unwritten "out of consideration for my father, for my mother, for myself" (140). He has written enough, however, to indicate that his father, with help from Okane and his wife, has carefully nurtured Tadasu's ability to distinguish between his two mothers, and has encouraged a sexual relationship between Tadasu and his stepmother, in preparation for Tadasu's taking his father's place in her life. What remains uncertain is whether a sexual relationship actually exists, and who Takeshi's father is.

Tadasu offers a number of clues relating to the last question. First, he says that his father "may well have thought it wrong for him to beget any other child than the one [his first wife] left him,"[13] implying that his father may not have begotten Takeshi. Second, there are rumors of an incestuous relationship between Tadasu and his stepmother. "According to them, Okane said, Mother and I began carrying on that way while Father was still alive, and Father himself, once he knew he wouldn't recover, had tolerated it—even encouraged it" (152). Third, "Some went so far as to ask whose baby had been smuggled out to Tamba, suggesting that Takeshi was my own child, not my father's" (152). Fourth, Tadasu does not deny these rumors but asks, in effect, how the truth got out ("I wondered how . . . these people . . . could have heard anything that would make them spread such wild rumors" [153]). Finally, he confirms that he has spent many hours alone with his stepmother and, at the same time, passes up another opportunity to deny the rumors (153). Taken together, these hints suggest that Tadasu has had a sexual relationship with his stepmother, that the relationship begins while his father is still alive and has his blessing, and that Tadasu is indeed Takeshi's father.

The beginning of the relationship can be dated to the period of seventeen or eighteen months between spring, 1923, when Tadasu begins to think of Tsuneko as an individual, and August or September, 1924, when Takeshi is conceived. It is already underway, then, before his father sets his plan in motion (in late October, 1924). It is probably Tadasu's physical relationship with Tsuneko and her pregnancy that encourage Father to think of Tadasu's taking his place.

Arrowroot, The Reed Cutter, and *Captain Shigemoto's Mother* each depicts a son who, at least psychologically, takes his father's place, and *Shigemoto* exemplifies the often-recurring motif of one man yielding his wife to another man; but nowhere else in Tanizaki's works are these themes so explicit, and the father-son identification so complete, as in *The Bridge of Dreams.* Not only does Tadasu look just like his father, he is specifically charged by his dying father to take his place: "What worries me most is your poor stepmother. She still has a long life ahead of her, but once I'm gone she'll have only you to rely on. So please take good care of her—give her all your love. Everyone says you resemble me. I think so myself. As you get older you'll look even more like me. If she has you, she'll feel as if I am still alive. I want you to think of taking my place with her as your chief aim in life, as the only kind of happiness you need" (144).

Part of Father's plan "to create a deeper intimacy" between Tadasu and his stepmother, "so that she would think of me as taking his place," calls for Tadasu to relive his "warm, dimly white dream world" with her. The implication is that Father, too, feels like a child when he is in his wife's arms, and if Tadasu is to take his place, he too must return to that state of mind. At the same time, Father encourages Tadasu to distinguish between his mother and his stepmother. Eagerly following his instructions, Tadasu takes a nominal wife to help him make his stepmother happy (recalling Seribashi's marriage to Oshizu, in *The Reed Cutter*), cools beer under the bamboo mortar as his father has done, and—we must assume—in every way takes his father's place in his stepmother's life. Tsuneko has evolved from an unindividualized Ideal Mother to a particular mother-wife-lover; and Tadasu, having started out as a child who adores an idealized Mother, grows into a man who fills the inherited roles of lover and husband while he continues also to play the role of child. "To please Mother," he says about his wedding, "I wore a crested black silk kimono of Father's instead of a morning coat" (154).[14]

Tadasu's references to *The Tale of Genji* suggest another perspective from which to examine his relationship with Tsuneko. The title of the novella, being the same as the title of the last chapter of the *Genji,* encourages the reader to look for connections. "The floating bridge of dreams" is a metaphor for the dreamlike quality of life and of the world of love.[15] As a title, the phrase also reinforces the view that Tadasu lives in a world of dreams, and it endows Tadasu's bridges (one at the front gate, the other spanning the pond) with symbolic significance. Ultimately, the title of the novella is an allusion to the entire *Tale of Genji.* As Tadasu says about his mother's poem, "The line 'I crossed the Bridge of Dreams' must mean 'Today I read "The Bridge of Dreams"–the last chapter of *The Tale of Genji.*' Since that is only a short chapter, one that would take very little time to read, no doubt she is saying that today she at last finished the whole of *Genji*" (97). For a reader who recognizes the parallels between the two works, a knowledge of the *Genji* and a reading of *The Bridge of Dreams* merge into a single, new perception, richer and more complex than would otherwise be possible, just as with allusive variation in Japanese poetry.[16] The parallels are striking.

Tadasu's circumstances recall those of Genji, whose mother dies when he is three years old and is replaced in the affections of both Genji and his father (the emperor) by Fujitsubo:

> [Genji] could not remember his own mother and it moved him deeply to learn . . . that the resemblance was striking. He wanted to be near her always.
>
> "Do not be unfriendly," said the emperor to Fujitsubo. "Sometimes it almost seems to me too that you are his mother. Do not think him forward, be kind to him. Your eyes, your expression: you are really so uncommonly like her that you could pass for his mother."[17]

In the story line that Tanizaki had to omit from his first *Genji* translation, the eighteen-year-old Genji has a sexual relationship with his stepmother Fujitsubo. She gives birth to a child, the future Reizei emperor, who is thought by everyone to be the son of Genji's father (though Genji later suspects that his father knew the truth). The parallel is inescapable: Tadasu (who is eighteen when Takeshi is conceived) corresponds to Genji, his stepmother to Fujitsubo, and Takeshi to Reizei. The close resemblance makes almost irresistible the conclusion that Tadasu is Takeshi's father.

Only four months after Takeshi's birth, Father is dead and Tadasu's world changes again. At first everyone seems content with the new routine. Tadasu plays his father's role, cooling beer under the water mortar, and the seasonal cycle resumes its flow: "A month or two after the silk-tree and pomegranate blossoms had fallen, when the crape myrtle was beginning to bloom and the plantain ripening, I had become fairly skillful at massaging and often asked Mother to come out to the pavilion for a treatment" (150). Cracks begin to appear in Tadasu's world shortly after he marries Sawako. Tadasu's assertion that "[o]n the surface, Mother appeared to get along with her newly wed son and daughter-in-law in perfect harmony" (154) hints at disharmony. One cause of tension is that Tsuneko "was especially strict with Sawako and caused her a good deal of worry over the food bills" (155). A frugal, strict, self-indulgent woman on the threshold of middle age, "almost too plump" (155), Tsuneko is losing the ability to be a springboard for Tadasu's fantasies as she becomes ever more of an individual and less like the Ideal Mother. Ironically, she threatens to become an obstacle to Tadasu's desire to maintain his dream world.

Sawako is even more out of place in Tadasu's world. She is an outsider—an inhabitant of the mundane world beyond Heron's Nest. She is "too reserved" for Tadasu's taste, "too solicitous," insincere, "curiously old-fashioned"—in a word, "inadequate" (150). He knows that his relatives suspect Sawako and her father of being after his property, and he has married her only because his father has told him that he would need someone to help make his stepmother happy. Sawako, too, stands between Tadasu and his fantasy.

If Tadasu is going to regain his dream world, then, he must be rid of both Tsuneko and Sawako and find someone else who can evoke fantasies of his Ideal Mother. It is Tadasu himself who first raises the possibility that his stepmother's death is a homicide. "I cannot escape certain nagging doubts," he says, ". . . [a]nd so I wonder if Mother's death was entirely accidental. Might not someone have had a scheme in mind for using a centipede, if one of them appeared? Perhaps it was only a rather nasty joke, with no thought that a mere insect bite could be fatal. But supposing that her weak heart had been taken into account, that the possibility had seemed attractive. . . . Even if the scheme failed, no one could prove that the centipede had been deliberately caught and placed there" (156–157). This is enough to arouse the suspicions of a reader who has encountered similar hints in other Tanizaki works. Tadasu casts suspicion on his wife: "It was odd that Sawako happened to see the insect—surely it would have been crawling under the kimono, out of sight. Perhaps she knew it was there" (158). Some readers have agreed with him. Sawako has reason to be jealous of her stepmother and probably wants to take charge of the household accounts. But a case can be made against Tadasu, as well.[18]

There is reason to suspect Tadasu of conspiring with Sawako to murder Tsuneko, by appealing to Sawako's greed and exploiting her jealousy and resentment. "A number of difficult conditions were proposed by her family," he says, "and in the end I had to agree to their terms" (158). If Sawako alone were responsible for Tsuneko's death, Tadasu could divorce her on his own terms. It must be because Sawako's family is in a position to blackmail him that he finally has to agree to their conditions; and the blackmail must be for something other than his "incestuous" relationship with his stepmother, since that relationship is already known to Tadasu's neighbors and relatives. The two years that elapse between Tsuneko's death and Tadasu's divorce can be accounted for by the difficulty of his negotiations with Sawako's family; it does not take him that long to realize that she has no place in his dream world.

In the last analysis, it is not clear whether Tsuneko's death is deliberate. Ambiguity prevails, as in *The Reed Cutter* and *A Portrait of Shunkin.* Whatever the case, however, Tadasu needs someone in Tsuneko's place to kindle his fantasies. That person is Takeshi. He looks like his mother (this is what makes Tadasu happiest), shares her temperament, and is only six years old—young enough to be malleable. Here, too, *The Bridge of Dreams* echoes *The Tale of Genji.* Genji's proclivity for pursuing likenesses of his mother draws him not only to Fujitsubo, but also to the motherless child Murasaki, because she resembles Fujitsubo. Appealing to Murasaki's grandmother, Genji says, "I have heard the sad story, and wonder if I might offer myself as a substitute for your late daughter [Murasaki's mother]. I was very young when I lost the one who was dearest to me [his own mother], and all through the years since I have had strange feelings of aimlessness and futility. We share the same fate, and I wonder if I might not ask that we be companions in it."[19] Brushing aside her nurse's objections, he takes the reluctant Murasaki from the hills north of Kyoto to his mansion in the city, where he rears and ultimately marries her. In a striking parallel, Tadasu is drawn to Takeshi because "he looks exactly like Mother," and he wants to take the place of the child's mother (159).[20] Tadasu's words echo Genji's: "Because my real mother died when I was a child, and my father and stepmother when I was some years older, I want to live for Takeshi until he is grown. I want to spare him the loneliness I knew" (159).

Like Genji, Tadasu insists on bringing Takeshi back from the hills north of Kyoto to live with him in the city, "in spite of his own reluctance as well as that of his foster parents" (158). Murasaki's nurse comes to live with her and Genji; Tadasu's nurse comes to help rear Takeshi. Takeshi's resemblance to Murasaki even extends to his "calm, open, generous temperament" (159). Takeshi, then, corresponds not only to Genji's son Reizei, but to Murasaki as well, and the implication is that Tadasu will live with Takeshi, as Genji does with Murasaki, as both parent and lover.[21]

More than one young man in the *Genji* substitutes a boy for the woman he loves. Genji does so with the brother of the Lady of the Locust Shell and finds the boy "more attractive than his chilly sister."[22] Another is Genji's putative son Kaoru. Infatuated with Oigimi, Kaoru turns to her younger sisters when she dies, especially to Ukifune, because she reminds him so much of Oigimi. At the end of the *Genji*, in "The Floating Bridge of Dreams," Kaoru, still longing for the inaccessible Ukifune, comforts himself by keeping her handsome brother beside him, because the boy resembles his sister.

At the end of *The Bridge of Dreams*, Tadasu has transcended all obstacles and reanimated his dream world by bringing Takeshi to live with him as son and brother, and possibly as lover, his "one link with Mother" (159), his "floating bridge of dreams" to Mother.[23]

Notes

List of Works Cited

Index

Notes

PREFACE

1. The essays here supersede what I have written about some of these works before. Important Tanizaki novels and novellas that I have not emphasized in this study include *Chijin no ai* (Naomi, 1924–1925), *Tade kuu mushi* (Some Prefer Nettles, 1928–1929), *Manji* (Quicksand, 1928–1930), *Mōmoku monogatari* (A Blind Man's Tale, 1931) *Neko to Shōzō to futari no onna* (A Cat, a Man, and Two Women, 1936), *Kagi* (The Key, 1956), and *Fūten rōjin nikki* (Diary of a Mad Old Man, 1961–1962). For discussions of all but two of these—*Mōmoku monogatari* and *Neko to Shōzō to futari no onna*—the reader is referred to Ken Ito's study of Tanizaki, *Visions of Desire*. Tanizaki's plays, essays, and poetry have so far received little attention in either English or Japanese.
2. *Tanizaki Jun'ichirō zenshū* (Chūō Kōronsha, 1966–1968) is, in fact, not "complete." Several early works have turned up since it was issued, and many letters and notebooks remain unpublished.
3. Donald Keene, *Dawn to the West*, p. 721.
4. Tanizaki Jun'ichirō, "Postscript to 'A Portrait of Shunkin,'" tr. Anthony H. Chambers, p. 463.

1. IDEAL WORLDS

1. Tanizaki Jun'ichirō, *Childhood Years: A Memoir*, tr. Paul McCarthy, p. 175. Tanizaki first tasted these pleasures at the age of eleven, when he read Iwaya Sazanami's *New Hakkenden*.
2. The theme of alternative worlds in Tanizaki's fiction was suggested thirty years ago by Howard Hibbett when he wrote, "Dreams, daydreams, elaborate fantasies—often dramatizing the secret affinity of love and cruelty—have had a significant place in Tanizaki's fiction ever since he began writing short stories in his twenties" ("Introduction" to Tani-

zaki Jun'ichirō, *Seven Japanese Tales,* tr. Howard Hibbett, p. vi). Makoto Ueda emphasizes the significance of the imagination for Tanizaki in his *Modern Japanese Writers and the Nature of Literature.* Chiba Shunji has written on Tanizaki's idealism and Platonism in "'Aozuka-shi no hanashi' ni tsuite: Taishō kara Shōwa e no Tanizaki Jun'ichirō" and in *Tanizaki Jun'ichirō.* Most recently, Ken Ito's *Visions of Desire: Tanizaki's Fictional Worlds* is, like the present study, concerned with characters who attempt "to bring into being a private realm apart from the given world" (Ito, p. 3); but Ito's emphasis is on the "problematics of desire" and "the discourse of culture" in the depiction of these worlds, while mine is on the beauty and truth that characters find in them. Of the thirteen works given special attention in Ito's study and mine, only two—*Shunkinshō* and *Sasameyuki*—are discussed in both.

3. Tanizaki Jun'ichirō, *Diary of a Mad Old Man,* tr. Howard Hibbett, pp. 15–17, 33.
4. Tanizaki was introduced to "Platonic and Schopenhauerian idealism" between 1897 and 1901 by an unusually dedicated and erudite teacher. Tanizaki Jun'ichirō, *Childhood Years,* pp. 145 ff.
5. See Jay Rubin, *Injurious to Public Morals: Writers and the Meiji State,* on Tanizaki's encounters with government censorship.
6. Other examples are the protagonists of *Ashikari* (The Reed Cutter), *Shōshō Shigemoto no haha* (Captain Shigemoto's Mother), and *Yume no ukihashi* (The Bridge of Dreams).
7. They include characters in *Yoshino kuzu* (Arrowroot), *Bushūkō hiwa* (The Secret History of the Lord of Musashi), and *The Makioka Sisters.*
8. Tanizaki Jun'ichirō, *In Praise of Shadows,* tr. Thomas J. Harper and Edward G. Seidensticker, p. 42.
9. Ibid., p. 34.
10. I think of Tanizaki's writings as falling into four periods: early (before *Chijin no ai* [Naomi]); early-middle (*Naomi* through *Manji* [Quicksand] and *Tade kuu mushi* [Some Prefer Nettles]); middle (*Arrowroot* through *Neko to shōzō to futari no onna* [A Cat, a Man, and Two Women]) and late (*The Makioka Sisters* and after).
11. Other personal turning points include the 1923 earthquake (which drove Tanizaki from Tokyo) and the beginning of his friendship with Nezu Matsuko (the later Tanizaki Matsuko) in 1927.
12. Satō Haruo, *Satō Haruo zenshū,* 11:455. The poet and novelist Satō Haruo (1892–1964) was a close friend of Tanizaki's. He published his assessment in 1934.
13. Despite the common misconception that Tanizaki came to appreciate Japanese culture only after the earthquake drove him to western Japan in 1923, his interest in Japanese tradition, so apparent in *Arrowroot,* was

nothing new. Many of his earliest stories and plays are set in premodern Japan, from the Heian to the Tokugawa periods.

2. ARROWROOT

1. Kuzunoha is also the name by which the fox-mother is known.
2. The title "Yoshino kuzu" was one of Tanizaki's favorites (21:446). In addition to recalling the play *Kuzu no ha,* it evokes the Yoshino village of Kuzu, an ancient court ceremony, and the nō play *Kuzu;* but the primary meaning of *kuzu* is "arrowroot" (*Pueraria lobata*), a noted product of Yoshino, and the *kuzu* of the title is written with this character.
3. Minakami Tsutomu, "Tanizaki sensei no shokan: aru shuppansha shachō e no tegami o yomu, sono ni," pp. 206–207.
4. Ibid., p. 212. The letter is dated April, 1930.
5. Many readers have identified the narrator with Tanizaki himself, but the author establishes the narrator as an independent character. The narrator says that he has been to Yoshino twice before, once with his mother when he was very young, and once after his mother's death, when he was a college student. This account differs in every detail from the facts of Tanizaki's life. Tanizaki first visited Yoshino in 1922 with his wife and daughter, at the age of thirty-five, when his mother had been dead for five years. Tanizaki emphasized the point in a late essay: "The 'mother' who is mentioned in this work is the mother of Tsumura's friend, not my mother. My mother was born in Fukagawa, Edo, in 1864, and died in Kakigara-chō, Nihombashi, Tokyo, in 1917. A pure child of Edo, she never set foot in western Japan" (19:448–449).
6. The numbers following quotations from *Arrowroot* refer to the page numbers in Tanizaki Jun'ichirō, *The Secret History of the Lord of Musashi and Arrowroot,* tr. Anthony H. Chambers.
7. "Side-man" as a translation of *waki* was coined by Royall Tyler for his translations in *Pining Wind: A Cycle of Nō Plays* and *Granny Mountains: A Second Cycle of Nō Plays.*
8. This summary of the *jo-ha-kyū* rhythm and the translation of the terms are adapted from Earl Miner, et al., *The Princeton Companion to Classical Japanese Literature,* pp. 311–312.
9. Itō Sei (1905–1969), novelist and critic. *Tanizaki Jun'ichirō no bungaku,* p. 151.
10. Unlike the "sources" quoted in *Bushūkō hiwa* (The Secret History of the Lord of Musashi) and *Shunkinshō* (A Portrait of Shunkin), all the texts cited in *Arrowroot* are authentic.
11. The *michiyuki* also refers to the eighth-century anthology *Man'yōshū,* to a haiku by Yosa Buson (1716–1783), and to the puppet play *Imoseyama*

onna teikin (Mt. Imo and Mt. Se: An Exemplary Tale of Womanly Virtue [the subject of a book entitled *Theater as Music* by C. Andrew Gerstle, et al.]). *Futari Shizuka* has been translated by Jacqueline Mueller. One scholar has convincingly suggested that *Arrowroot* also contains an indirect allusion to Po Chü-i's *Song of Everlasting Sorrow* (Takakuwa Noriko, "*Yoshino kuzu* ron: gengoteki hokōsha no katari to shite," in Chiba Shunji, ed., *Tanizaki Jun'ichirō: monogatari no hōhō*, p. 145).

12. The fox theme recurs often in Tanizaki's writings. In *Yōshō jidai* (Childhood Years: A Memoir, 1955–1956) he writes at length on his childhood memories of the fox-plays *Arrowroot Leaves* and *The Thousand Cherry Trees*, and he devotes an entire section of the autobiographical essay *Setsugoan yawa* (An Evening Chat at Setsugoan, 1963–1964) to his memories of the latter play (19:448–459). In the essay *Jōzetsuroku* (Babblings) he recalls being impressed by the puppet play *Nijūshikō no kitsunebi*, in which Princess Yaegaki is possessed by a fox (20:130). In his 1923 play *Byakko no yu* (White Fox Hot Spring, translated as The White Fox), a young man living in a mountain village is possessed and killed by a fox disguised as an alluring foreign lady (8:473–502). This play, too, was influenced by *The Thousand Cherry Trees* (19:456). In the brief "Kiinokuni no kitsune urushikaki ni tsuku monogatari" (A Fox Bewitches a Lacquer-gatherer in the Province of Kii," 1931), a group of foxes bewitch a peasant, but the victim is lucky enough to escape and tell the tale (13:159–172). Finally, Naomi (in *Chijin no ai* [Naomi, 1924–1925]) and other Tanizaki *femmes fatales* are occasionally likened to foxes. The prominent Tanizaki scholar Chiba Shunji has focused on the fox motif in three recent articles, including his commentary "Kitsune no shūjigaku" (Fox Rhetoric), in Chiba Shunji, ed., *Tanizaki Jun'ichirō: monogatari no hōhō*, pp. 248–257.

13. For this insight, and for some of the details given below in support of it, I am indebted to Ōhashi Takahiko, "*Yoshino kuzu* no sekai," pp. 197–213.

3. THE SECRET HISTORY OF THE LORD OF MUSASHI

1. See Howard Hibbett's translation in Tanizaki Jun'ichirō, *Seven Japanese Tales*, pp. 205–298.
2. Itō Sei, "Kaisetsu," p. 182.
3. The letter is published in Hata Kōhei, *Kami to gangu to no aida*, p. 154.
4. Edward Seidensticker, *Tokyo Rising*, p. 16.
5. Itō, *Tanizaki Jun'ichirō no bungaku*, p. 139. Among the important writers who emerged in response to this need were Nakazato Kaizan (1885–1944), Naoki Sanjūgo (1891–1934), Yoshikawa Eiji (1892–1962), and Osaragi Jirō (1897–1973).

6. Tanizaki read Stendhal and other French authors in English translation.
7. Ibuki Kazuko, personal letter, December 7, 1973.
8. Cited in Chiba Shunji, "Tanizaki Jun'ichirō *Bushūkō hiwa* ni tsuite," p. 200. Tanizaki missed the deadline; serialization actually began in October.
9. Cited in Nomura Shōgo, *Tanizaki Jun'ichirō no sakuhin*, p. 170.
10. *Shinseinen*, February, 1933, p. 225.
11. Chiba, "*Bushūkō hiwa* ni tsuite," pp. 199–200.
12. For example, the celebrated *yomihon*, *Ugetsu monogatari* (Tales of Moonlight and Rain, 1776) by Ueda Akinari (1734–1809).
13. Cited in Chiba, "*Bushūkō hiwa* ni tsuite," p. 203.
14. The numbers following references to and quotations from the text of *The Secret History* refer to the page numbers in Tanizaki Jun'ichirō, *The Secret History of the Lord of Musashi and Arrowroot*, tr. Anthony H. Chambers.
15. Nomura Shōgo, *Tanizaki Jun'ichirō: fūdo to bungaku*, p. 160.
16. Ibuki, personal letter, December 7, 1973.
17. Though some details are obscure, the gist of the outline is clear enough. A central player in the first half is Oura, the daughter of Norishige and Lady Kikyō. After her father's death (according to the outline), she sees his face for the first time and hears the story of his missing nose from her mother. Lady Kikyō commits suicide. Dōami shows Norishige's nose to Oura, who resolves to avenge her father. Meanwhile, Matoba Shinzaburō, the youngest son of Lady Kikyō's nurse, learns that it was none other than the Lord of Musashi who took Yakushiji's nose at the siege of Ojika Castle. Determined to kill the lord, Shinzaburō abducts Oura and flees.

    In the second half of the outline, Terukatsu finds Oteru (the girl he sees dressing a woman-head in the novel's most memorable scene) and marries her. Training Ohisa (Shōsetsuin's loveliest attendant) as her accomplice, Oteru plots against her new husband. (The outline does not explain her motives.) Oteru and Ohisa practice on Dōami, baiting him, cutting off his left ear, and finally castrating him. Dōami warns his master of their plans, but to no avail. In the end, the Lord of Musashi himself is castrated.
18. Noses figure in a number of earlier Tanizaki works, as well. A prostitute's nose stirs a young artist's dormant lust in the story "Hyōfu" (Blizzards, 1911), and pulls him back again and again, just as Terukatsu is pulled to the heads in the attic:

    > When, drawing strength from his drunkenness, he finally lost his virginity after more than twenty years, his only reaction, aside from a satisfied curiosity, was a feeling that the woman's nostrils, viewed from below, had something a little ominous about them. Nevertheless, he had a strange urge to visit her again—twice, three

times—until presently he began to be drawn by the very nostrils that he had thought merely odd before.

(1:212)

In *Chijin no ai* (Naomi), too, the heroine's nose engenders mixed feelings of longing and repulsion; and Tadasu, the narrator of *Yume no ukihashi* (The Bridge of Dreams), peers up at his mother's nostrils while he nurses.

Boys' noses, in contrast, are objects of other males' contempt and ridicule. In the story "Zōnen" (Hatred, 1914), for example:

> From where I stood, . . . I could clearly see Yasutarō's nostrils. "What ugly, filthy nostrils," I said to myself. I gazed at the bridge of his nose: it flattened as his face contorted with pain. "Why must human faces have nostrils?" I thought. "They'd look better without them."
>
> Before long, a maid intervened and stopped the quarrel; but I couldn't forget those nostrils for many days after. . . . "What a miserable wretch you are," I muttered whenever I saw Yasutarō. "Hideous. Just look at that ugly nose." We'd been close friends before, but now, for no reason at all, I was filled with loathing whenever I thought of that nose.

(2:293–294)

The play *Udezumō* (Arm wrestling, 1924) presents four university students arm-wrestling with each other at a hot spring, where they are supposed to be studying for exams. The penalty for losing is to have one's nose painted with black ink. Three of the students devise a plan to paint the fourth's nose with indelible dye instead, which, they imagine, will embarrass him in front of his girlfriend. This prank recalls the Heian courtier Heichū moistening his cheeks with water to make the lady he is visiting think he has been weeping; she foils his strategy by adding ink to the water. (The incident is mentioned in *Captain Shigemoto's Mother.*) It also recalls the passage at the end of Chapter Six of *The Tale of Genji* (which itself alludes to the Heichū story), where Genji playfully paints his nose red and teases Murasaki, his wife-to-be.

19. The term *onnakubi* (woman-head) originally referred to a nose or ear taken on the battlefield and presented as evidence when there had been no time to take an enemy's head. In such a case, a warrior was supposed to take part of the upper lip and mustache with the nose, to prove that it had come from the head of a warrior, and not from a woman or a priest. *Onnakubi* was one of four categories of dubious heads. The others were *tsukurikubi* (made-up heads), which had been altered to look like someone else; *sutekubi* (abandoned heads), left behind on the field by a victorious warrior and later picked up by someone else; and *yamaikubi* (disabled heads), taken from an enemy who had already been wounded by someone other than the warrior who claimed the head. In each case, leaders had to exercise special care to avoid giving credit where none was due.

20. Tanizaki Jun'ichirō, *Childhood Years*, p. 97.
21. Masamune Hakuchō (1879–1962), novelist and critic. "*Bushūkō hiwa* atogaki," in *Masamune Hakuchō zenshū*, 6:364.
22. Chiba, "*Bushūkō hiwa* ni tsuite," p. 205. Kokingo is a loyal retainer of the defeated Koremori. Not yet having been initiated into adulthood, Kokingo still has his boyish forelocks. He has escorted Koremori's wife, Wakaba no Naishi, and son, Rokudai, to Shimoichi in Yoshino. They are attacked. Naishi and Rokudai escape, but the young Kokingo dies defending them. His body is found by Yazaemon, the proprietor of the *sushi* shop where Koremori is hiding. Yazaemon takes Kokingo's head, intending to pass it off as Koremori's. After some complications, Kokingo's head is presented to the shōgun's emissary (it is a *tsukurikubi*, its forelocks cut off to make it look like an adult's head). After conducting a formal inspection, the emissary accepts the head as Koremori's, and so in the end Kokingo's self-sacrifice saves Koremori, Naishi, and Rokudai.
23. The passage from *Oan monogatari* is quoted by Donald Keene in his "Kaisetsu," p. 555. Tanizaki probably saw prints illustrating this passage, as well. One of them, reproduced in Keene's "Kaisetsu," depicts three gorgeously attired women servicing an assortment of severed heads. A different illustration appears in Kōno Toshirō, et al., "Tanizaki no sakuhin o yominaosu," p. 106.
24. Ibuki, personal letter, December 7, 1973.
25. Murasaki Shikibu, *The Tale of Genji*, tr. Edward G. Seidensticker, p. 158.
26. In view of Tanizaki's fondness for identifying his third wife, Matsuko, with Fujitsubo and Murasaki, it is tempting to agree with Hata Kōhei that there may be something of Matsuko in Lady Kikyō, and of Tanizaki's second wife, Tomiko, in Shōsetsuin. Hata has argued that the roles of Shōsetsuin and Kikyō reflect Tanizaki's 1931 relationship with his first wife (Chiyo), his second wife (Tomiko), and his third-wife-to-be, Matsuko. Hata's argument, though marred by dubious logic ("who can say for sure that it is not so?"), is, by and large, convincing. According to Hata, Tanizaki's unhappy first and second marriages are reflected in Terukatsu's relationship with Shōsetsuin, and Tanizaki's love for Matsuko is reflected in Terukatsu's adoration of Kikyō. Shōsetsuin, unable or unwilling to go along with her husband's "games," corresponds most closely to Tomiko, who lacked the "theatricality" necessary to maintain a successful marriage with Tanizaki. Lady Kikyō, on the other hand, plays along and helps Terukatsu fulfill his fantasies—like Matsuko, she has a good sense of theater. When the novel was first written and serialized, however, Matsuko was still married to her first husband and seemed inaccessible to Tanizaki. Tanizaki's frustration and feelings of

rivalry are reflected, Hata suggests, in Terukatsu's cruel treatment of Norishige; and Tanizaki's belief that Matsuko was beyond his reach is reflected in Lady Kikyō's change of heart in the Third Valley Palace. While there may be some truth in all of this, I doubt that the personal factor was as decisive in the planning and writing of *The Secret History* as Hata maintains. The pitfalls of biographical criticism aside (and some Japanese scholars have faulted Western scholars of Japanese literature for not paying more attention to biographical considerations), Hata's analysis fails to account for Tanizaki's continuing desire to write a sequel to the novel after he had been married to Matsuko for twenty-five years. See Hata, *Kami to gangu to no aida,* especially pp. 158–159.

27. The sentiment is echoed in *Shōshō Shigemoto no haha* (Captain Shigemoto's Mother, 1949–1950): Shigemoto's belief that he takes after his father and is ugly enhances the beauty of his mother as he imagines her. Similarly, the old man in *Fūten rōjin nikki* (Diary of a Mad Old Man, 1961–1962) compares his own appearance with that of his daughter-in-law: "The uglier the face in the mirror, the more extraordinarily beautiful Satsuko seemed." Tanizaki Jun'ichirō, *Diary of a Mad Old Man,* p. 101.

28. Tanizaki's aversion to the military (the self-proclaimed modern heirs to the samurai tradition) is well known. In his very first story, published in a middle-school literary magazine, he wrote: "Ever since I was a small child I had disliked military men most of all human beings, and businessmen next" (24:76, translated by Donald Keene in *Dawn to the West,* p. 724).

29. The original inspiration for this scene may have been something that happened to Tanizaki's mother. As he describes it in *Childhood Years:* "Once, late at night, Mother came rushing out of the toilet screaming for Father to come quickly. . . . It seemed that when Mother entered the water closet she found a strange man trying to crawl up into the room from the pit beneath—reason enough to flee screaming. But when my father went to look, there was no trace of anyone. Mother kept trying to explain what had happened: a hand had suddenly emerged from below, she said. . . . At any rate, the strange creature apparently had fled on hearing my mother's screams. My parents seemed to think he was not just a common thief or burglar. . . . Now, of course, I realize it must have been the act of a pervert." Tanizaki Jun'ichirō, *Childhood Years,* pp. 69–70.

30. The sharpest barb of all is untranslatable. The last phrase in this passage, *shin ni mojidōri kambashii saigo o togeta no de arō* (13:278; more precisely translated, "truly, he met a literally *kambashii* end"), includes a cruel pun on *kambashii,* which means, primarily, "fragrant," and by exten-

sion, "splendid." Further, since *kambashii* is most commonly used to modify *hana* (flower), which is homophonic with *hana* (nose), the jab at samurai devotion is also a reminder of Terukatsu's and Kikyō's unusual obsessions.

31. Murasaki, p. 437.

4. THE REED CUTTER

1. Satō, *Satō Haruo zenshū*, 11:463. Satō (1892–1964), poet and novelist; Kubota (1889–1963), dramatist, novelist, poet.
2. Tanizaki Jun'ichirō, *Ashikari and the Story of Shunkin*, tr. Roy Humpherson and Hajime Okita.
3. The numbers following quotations from *The Reed Cutter* refer to the page numbers in Tanizaki Jun'ichirō, *The Reed Cutter and Captain Shigemoto's Mother: Two Novellas*, tr. Anthony H. Chambers.
4. *Yamato monogatari* has been translated by Mildred M. Tahara. The nō *Ashikari* appears as *The Reed Cutter*, tr. James A. O'Brien, in *Twenty Plays of the Nō Theatre*, ed. Donald Keene, pp. 147–164. Hiroko Kobayashi provides a translation of the *Konjaku* version and discusses its relationship to a number of other versions in *The Human Comedy of Heian Japan*, pp. 216–247. See also Marian Ury's translation in *Tales of Times Now Past*, pp. 192–194.
5. Some texts have "omou ni wa" in place of "omou ni mo," and "ura zo" instead of "ura wa." The wording given here is that used by Tanizaki. The title "Ashikari" is derived from this poem, in which "ashikarikeri," "how wretched," contains the homophonous "ashikari," "reed cutting" or "reed cutter."
6. Two well known expressions of the more common paradigm are the nō play *Kinuta* and the tale "Asaji ga yado" (The House Amid the Thickets) in *Ugetsu monogatari. Kinuta* is available in translations by the Nippon Gakujutsu Shinkōkai, *Japanese Noh Drama*, III, pp. 113–132; by Tyler in *Pining Wind*, pp. 155–170, under the title *The Block;* and by Eileen Katō. The best available translation of "Asaji ga yado" is Leon Zolbrod's, in Ueda Akinari, *Ugetsu Monogatari: Tales of Moonlight and Rain*, pp. 121–132.
7. Hata Kōhei, "Oyūsama: waga Tanizaki no *Ashikari* kō," pp. 220–240. Reprinted in Hata, *Tanizaki Jun'ichirō:* Genji monogatari *taiken*, pp. 75–126.
8. To be more exact, "when Miss Oyū was in her twenty-fourth or twenty-fifth year."
9. Oyū's twenty-seventh or twenty-eighth year would coincide with her new son's first year; he was in his seventh or eighth year when he first

went to the villa with his father, and so now is in his forty-seventh, -eighth, or -ninth; thus 26 + 47 = 73, the youngest she could be, and 27 + 49 = 76, the oldest.

10. The above nine paragraphs summarize the important points of Hata's article.
11. Robert H. Brower and Earl Miner, *Japanese Court Poetry*, p. 506.
12. See, for example, the postscript to Takeuchi Kiyomi's "Tanizaki Jun'ichirō *Ashikari* ron: sono kokubungakuteki kōzō."
13. Hata Kōhei cites the lack of a dramatic flair as a shortcoming shared by Terukatsu's wife Shōsetsuin, in *The Secret History*, and Tanizaki's second wife Tomiko. See Chapter Three, note 26.
14. *Kogō*, by Komparu Zenchiku (1405–?), is based on an episode in the thirteenth-century *Heike monogatari* (The Tale of the Heike), Book 6, Chapter 4.
15. Two letters from Tanizaki to Matsuko are of great interest for what they say about Matsuko's role as the inspiration for Oyū. In 1932 or 1933 (the letter is undated), he wrote: "I am sending you the *Genji kogetsushō* [the 1673 commentary on the *Genji*, by Kitamura Kigin] and the second volume of the modern translation. I doubt that anyone today is as well suited to read the *Genji* as you. It is as if the *Genji* had been written simply that you might read it." Several years later, after he had begun his own translation of the *Genji* into modern Japanese, he wrote: "As I translate the *Genji*, images of you float up, one after another, before my eyes. The world of the *Genji* is your world." The letters are published in Tanizaki Matsuko, *Ishōan no yume*, pp. 214–215 and 216.
16. Edward Seidensticker, *This Country, Japan*, p. 66.
17. One commentator has pointed out that Oyū, seated in a room that has been built out over the garden pond, is also a *suijō no onna*, a woman on the water, like the floating courtesans. Miyauchi Junko, "Tanizaki Jun'ichirō *Ashikari Yume no ukihashi* nado," p. 154.
18. Both poems play on the multiple meanings of "kari no yadori," which signifies a temporary lodging, a rented lodging, and the body, a temporary repository of life. This exchange, with an explanatory headnote, is contained in the thirteenth-century anthology *Shinkokinshū* (nos. 978 and 979), where the woman is identified as "the courtesan Tai." It also appears (in slightly different form) in *Sankashū*, Saigyō's personal collection (poem nos. 820 and 821), and in the early-Kamakura *Senjūshō*, a *setsuwa* collection sometimes attributed to Saigyō. For a discussion of the Saigyō story from a different perspective, see William R. LaFleur, *The Karma of Words: Buddhism and the Literary Arts in Medieval Japan*, pp. 70–71.
19. 12:220. Similar accounts are contained in the thirteenth-century *setsuwa* collections *Kojidan* and *Jikkinshō*. The latter has been translated by John

Brownlee. See also Michele Marra, "The Buddhist Mythmaking of Defilement: Sacred Courtesans in Medieval Japan." On the sources for the nō *Eguchi,* see also Yokomichi Mario and Omote Akira, eds., *Yōkyokushū,* I, p. 49. The Samantabhadra legend is recounted by the *aikyōgen* on p. 53 of this edition.

20. Tyler, *Pining Wind,* p. 87.
21. There are other echoes of *Eguchi* in *The Reed Cutter,* as well. In the play, the courtesans, viewing the full moon of the Eighth Month from their pleasure boat, sing "Bubbles of froth, we'll tell, alas, our yearning love for long ago . . ." (Tyler, *Pining Wind,* p. 84), anticipating the narrator's nostalgia for the past, and even his imagery. In addition to Tyler's, there is a translation by the Nippon Gakujutsu Shinkōkai, in *Japanese Noh Drama,* I, pp. 107–124. My discussion of the play has benefitted from both translations and from Mikame Tatsuji's study, "Tanizaki no *Ashikari* ni okeru nōgakuteki kōsei."
22. Nippon Gakujutsu Shinkōkai, *Japanese Noh Drama,* I, p. 111.
23. Tyler, *Pining Wind,* p. 76.
24. The subject is treated at length by Saeki Junko in her *Yūjo no bunka shi.* One of the Lord of Musashi's biographers writes that he, too, may have been "a compassionate Buddha or Bodhisattva who, demonstrating in his own person the inexorable law of cause and effect and the cycle of transmigration, appeared in this world for a time to lead us out of illusion." Tanizaki Jun'ichirō, *The Secret History of the Lord of Musashi and Arrowroot,* p. 7.
25. *Taketori* has been translated by Donald Keene, in J. Thomas Rimer, *Modern Japanese Fiction and Its Traditions,* pp. 275–305.
26. Tanizaki Jun'ichirō, *Naomi,* tr. Anthony H. Chambers, p. 176; p. 210.
27. Tanizaki Jun'ichirō, *Some Prefer Nettles,* tr. Edward Seidensticker, p. 101; pp. 36–37.
28. The poem is the *Cheng tao ke,* by the T'ang poet-priest Hsüan Chüeh (also known as Yung-chia Ta-shih).
29. The translation is by Leon Zolbrod, in Ueda Akinari, pp. 192–193.
30. Several commentators have analyzed the man's role in these terms. One view is that he is possessed in the latter half of the novella by the spirit of Oyū, just as the *nochijite* of the play *Izutsu* is possessed by the spirit of her lover Narihira. (Noguchi Takehiko, *Tanizaki Jun'ichirō ron,* p. 206.) Another view is that the man is possessed by the ghost of his father. Tanizaki has adapted only the first half of the nō structure, according to this analysis: the man in the reeds is the *maejite,* and if the novella continued in the manner of a nō play he would reappear as *nochijite* in his father's form. (Fukuda Kiyoto and Hirayama Jōji, *Tanizaki Jun'ichirō: hito to sakuhin,* pp. 145–146.) One of my students has suggested that the

man in the reeds is the spirit of the narrator himself, or the embodiment of the narrator's fantasy to be a native of Osaka, not Tokyo. The man does resemble the shadow of the narrator of "Longing for Mother": "Tonight's moon is so lovely that I just had to come out," the shadow says, "and since you're here all alone, I thought I'd keep you company" (Tanizaki Jun'ichirō, "Longing for Mother," tr. Edward Fowler, p. 473). Another student, pointing out that the narrator dines on "two bowls of fox noodles (14) and mentions a nearby ferry crossing called "Kitsune no Watashi," or "Fox Crossing" (14), has suggested that the man in the reeds is a fox.

31. *Yuya* has been translated by the Nippon Gakujutsu Shinkōkai, *Japanese Noh Drama,* II, pp. 31–51; and by Tyler, in *Granny Mountains,* pp. 77–90.

5. A PORTRAIT OF SHUNKIN

1. Satō, *Satō Haruo zenshū,* 11:456; and Masamune Hakuchō, "*Shunkinshō* sono ta," p. 81. Masamune Hakuchō (1879–1962) was an important writer and critic; his essay was originally published in September, 1933.
2. Yabe Ryōsaku, "*Shunkinshō* zengo no omoide," p. 5.
3. *Satō Haruo zenshū,* 11:467–468.
4. Tanizaki Matsuko, personal interview, March 28, 1981. Schnitzler was introduced to the Japanese public through translations by Mori Ōgai (1862–1922) and Yamamoto Yūzō (1887–1974). Yūzō's 1921 translation of "The Blind Geronimo and His Brother" attracted the attention of the great kabuki actor Onoe Kikugorō VI (1885–1949), who urged Yūzō to adapt the story to a play with a Japanese setting. In 1929 Yūzō responded with *Mōmoku no otōto* (The Blind Little Brother), which Kikugorō produced and starred in the following year.
5. Arthur Schnitzler, *The Shepherd's Pipe and Other Stories,* tr. O. F. Theis, pp. 148–150. Tanizaki may have known the story through this 1922 translation, as well as through Yūzō's.
6. Schnitzler, p. 160.
7. This is true of Yūzō's dramatization, as well: Kikugorō starred as Carlo, not as Geronimo.
8. Schnitzler, pp. 125, 163.
9. Schnitzler, p. 169.
10. The numbers following quotations from *A Portrait of Shunkin* refer to the page numbers in Howard Hibbett's translation (in Tanizaki Jun'ichirō, *Seven Japanese Tales,* pp. 3–84).
11. Thomas Hardy, *A Group of Noble Dames,* p.77.
12. I am indebted to Chiba Shunji for bringing these plays to my attention. See his *Tanizaki Jun'ichirō,* p. 159.

13. Hardy, p. 110.
14. Tanizaki Jun'ichirō, *The Secret History of the Lord of Musashi and Arrowroot,* p. 141. Another parallel between "Barbara" and *The Secret History* is too striking to omit. Willowes's mutilated statue, "with a wax-candle burning on each side of it to throw the cropped and distorted features into relief" (Hardy, p. 114), is echoed no less than three times in Tanizaki's novel. Masataka's face, illuminated by flickering lamp light, encites Hōshimaru; Norishige's face is similarly lit as Terukatsu spies on him; and Dōami imitates a woman-head with "lamps placed on either side of [his] head" as Terukatsu and Shōsetsuin watch from bed.
15. Satō Haruo and later commentators have found other parallels between "Barbara" and *Shunkin,* including similarities in the narrative technique, the superior social status of the woman in each case, and the role of blindness. See, for example, Ōta Saburō, "Thomas Hardy to Tanizaki Jun'ichirō: *Shunkinshō* o meguru mondai," pp. 151–153; and Anthony V. Liman, "The True Mark of a Saint," pp. 103–106.
16. Seidensticker, *Tokyo Rising,* p. 98.
17. The references appear in *Tanizaki Jun'ichirō zenshū,* 13:533, 498, and 515, respectively, and are included in Tanizaki Jun'ichirō, *Ashikari and the Story of Shunkin,* pp. 133, 77, and 102, respectively, but are omitted from Hibbett's translation. They do not, of course, indicate that the narrator is Tanizaki himself. Like the narrators of *Arrowroot, The Secret History of the Lord of Musashi,* and *The Reed Cutter,* the narrator of *Shunkin* is a fictional creation. Maeda Hisanori analyzes the relationship between the narrator and the author in *Shunkin* in "Monogatari no kōzō," especially pp. 98–100.
18. Many of these reminders (and the title "Kengyō") are diluted or omitted in Hibbett's translation. For example, a more literal rendering of the passage quoted above might conclude: "Osaka has changed almost beyond recognition since *Kengyō's* day, but these two stones still testify to *the deep bond between teacher and pupil*" (13:496, emphasis added).
19. Satō, *Satō Haruo zenshū,* 11:466.
20. To the last phrase I have restored the word "ideal" [*kannen no*] from the original (13:552).
21. Chiba Shunji has traced Sasuke's concentration on an "ideal Shunkin" in preference to the "real Shunkin" to Tanizaki's interest in the Platonic theory of eternal Ideas or Forms. Chiba finds earlier reflections of this interest in such works as "Ave Maria" (1923), "Nikukai" (A Lump of Flesh, 1923), and "Aozuka-shi no hanashi" (The Story of Mr. Aozuka, 1926), and suggests that it finds its ultimate expression in *A Portrait of Shunkin.* Chiba, *Tanizaki Jun'ichirō,* pp. 159–160. See also Chiba's essay "'Aozuka-shi no hanashi' ni tsuite."

22. Noguchi, *Tanizaki Jun'ichirō ron,* p. 208.
23. Sugimori Hisahide, "Shunkinshō," p. 191.
24. Tanizaki Jun'ichirō, "Postscript to 'A Portrait of Shunkin,'" tr. Anthony H. Chambers, p. 462.
25. Quoted by Inazawa Hideo in *Tanizaki Jun'ichirō no sekai,* p. 63.
26. Though he does not mention them, Tanizaki uses several devices to compensate for the sparse punctuation in *A Portrait of Shunkin.* Passages from *The Life of Mozuya Shunkin* are set off from the surrounding narrative by virtue of being written in classical Japanese, just as direct quotations in Osaka dialect stand apart from the narrative, which is in modern Tokyo Japanese. Breaks between phrases and sentences within unpunctuated passages are frequently suggested by the use of *kana* at the end of a phrase and a Chinese character at the beginning of the next, a practice that produces an effect similar to that of capital letters in English.
27. "Essentialism" is my translation of *shai,* literally, "depiction of the heart (or essence)," and "Naturalisitic realism," of *shizenshugiteki shajitsu, shajitsu* being, literally, "depiction of reality." Satō, *Satō Haruo zenshū,* 11:464.
28. Hashimoto Yoshiichirō, *Tanizaki Jun'ichirō no bungaku,* p. 152.
29. Tanizaki Jun'ichirō, "Postscript," pp. 466, 464, 462.
30. Ibid., p. 464. Mark Twain said much the same thing: "I can't stand George Eliot and Hawthorne and those people. I see what they are at a hundred years before they get to it and they just tire me to death." (Quoted in the *Christian Science Monitor,* May 26, 1982.) In "Postscript," Tanizaki also writes, "I too used to think that a work which did not achieve verisimilitude in characterization and setting through dialogue was not a true novel. . . . It seemed to me that since anyone with a modicum of talent could manage the *monogatari* style or the essay style, a professional writer choosing that path must be cowardly and lazy. I have now abandoned this childish and absurd notion" (p. 463). This is a reversal of his position of only three years earlier. See the discussion of *Rangiku monogatari* (A Tale of Chrysanthemums in Chaos) in Chapter Three.
31. Noguchi, *Tanizaki Jun'ichirō ron,* p. 210.
32. Rimer, *Modern Japanese Fiction and Its Traditions,* p. 28.
33. Ōoka Shōhei, "*Shunkinshō kōgo* tokugokan," p. 251.
34. Tanizaki Jun'ichirō, "Postscript," p. 465.
35. Ibid., p. 466.
36. Noda Yoshio, for example, does so when he summarizes the novella in "Mōmoku monogatari, *Shunkinshō.*" Kubota Mantarō's 1935 stage adaptation has Sasuke grappling with the intruder; Shunkin is scalded when a kettle of hot water on her *hibachi* is overturned in their struggle.

(Cited in Nagae Hironobu, *Tanizaki Jun'ichirō shiron*, p. 66.)

37. Kōno Taeko, *Tanizaki bungaku to kōtei no yokubō*, p. 151.
38. Nosaka Akiyuki, "Shunkinshō," pp. 90–91.
39. The best presentation of the Sasuke-as-culprit theory (*Sasuke hannin setsu*) is Chiba Shunji's, in his *Tanizaki Jun'ichirō*, pp. 162–167. The theory can be summarized as follows. First, Sasuke's motive is his longing for an ideal world to live in with Shunkin, undisturbed by outside people and events. In the world he longs for, Shunkin's beauty would be unchanging, Sasuke himself would be blind, and the master-pupil relationship would continue unaltered. But time and events conspire against Sasuke. As Shunkin ages, her beauty will inevitably fade—so long as Sasuke depends on his eyes to perceive it. Nor is Sasuke without rivals, a fact that he realizes for the first time at Ritarō's party. The party also impresses upon Sasuke that his control over Shunkin is tenuous and that both he and Shunkin are potentially subject to manipulation by others. By disfiguring Shunkin and blinding himself, Sasuke would be able to eliminate his rivals and bind Shunkin to himself forever, remove his dependence on a visual appreciation of Shunkin's beauty (and thereby thwart the aging process), and enjoy "the quickening of that sixth sense which only the blind possess" (74), making new sensual delights possible.

    Ritarō's party and his subsequent encounter with Shunkin provide Sasuke with a perfect opportunity, since suspicion would focus on Ritarō. As an insider, Sasuke has many advantages. An outsider would have to "force open the shutters" (68) to get into the house—a noisy operation, as anyone who has lived in an old Japanese house can confirm. Further, no one is in as good a position as Sasuke to slip into the kitchen at night, build a fire, boil water, and enter Shunkin's room without waking Shunkin or the servants. (Any of the servants would have the same opportunity as Sasuke, but none of them is provided with a motive.)

    Nagae Hironobu, responding to Chiba, considers it more likely that Shunkin and Sasuke conspire together to disfigure Shunkin (*Tanizaki Jun'ichirō shiron*, pp. 65–80). Hata Kōhei, inspired by Nagae to respond to Chiba, insists that Shunkin disfigures herself (*Tanizaki Jun'ichirō*, pp. 191–232). Hata's argument makes little sense, however, as Chiba shows in his rebuttal ("Katari no nawa—Hata Kōhei 'Shunkin jigai' wo bakusu.") Maeda Hisanori, responding to Chiba, Nagae, and Hata, points out that nothing in the text is inconsistent with the narrator's conclusion that the culprit was an outsider, and urges us to accept this view ("Monogatari no kōzo"). Chiba himself is no longer interested in trying to identify Shunkin's attacker. "*A Portrait of Shunkin*," he says, "is not a detective novel" ("Katari no nawa," p. 9).

As far as I know, the only other treatment of the theory in English is by Ken Ito, in his *Visions of Desire*, pp. 179–180. "The theory's importance," Ito concludes, "rests not so much with proving Sasuke the villain, but in suggesting just how far a willful man may have gone in transforming another human being into his vision of the ideal."

40. The change occurs in *Zenshū* 13:503–504, which corresponds to Hibbett, p. 14.
41. Nosaka, pp. 90–91.
42. Tanizaki Jun'ichirō, *The Secret History of the Lord of Musashi and Arrowroot*, p. 63.
43. Tanizaki Jun'ichirō, *Naomi*, pp. 20–21.
44. Chiba, "Katari no nawa," p. 9. Liman moves in this direction in his "The True Mark of a Saint."

6. THE MAKIOKA SISTERS

1. Nakamura Shin'ichirō, "Tanizaki to *Sasameyuki*," p. 58.
2. Satō, *Satō Haruo zenshū*, 11:461. The translation is from Noguchi Takehiko, "Time in the World of *Sasameyuki*," tr. Teruko Craig, p. 7.
3. Satō, *Satō Haruo zenshū*, 11:462; Noguchi, "Time," p. 7.
4. Elsewhere he says, "In the case of *The Makioka Sisters*, unlike that of *Some Prefer Nettles*, I drew up a plan—I would begin this way, end that way, and so on—and in general the novel turned out as I planned" (22:366).
5. Jay Rubin gives a more detailed account of the government's actions in *Injurious to Public Morals*, pp. 263–265.
6. Edward Seidensticker recalls (in a personal correspondence of November 18, 1990) that there was an additional reason for discarding *San shimai:* there are four Makioka sisters, and "'four sisters' does not sound good in Japanese." The English title, Seidensticker writes, was coined by Harold Strauss, his editor at Knopf. "Tanizaki indicated oblique approval. It was very near a title he had considered himself [*San shimai*], he said, and reluctantly discarded."
7. On this subject I am indebted to Chiba Shunji, "*Sasameyuki* ron," in *Kokubungaku kaishaku to kanshō* 52:4 (April, 1987), pp. 131–144.
8. This recalls *Kokinshū* no. 9, "On Falling Snow," by Ki no Tsurayuki:

Kasumi tachi ko no me mo haru no yuki fureba
hana naki sato mo hana zo chirikeru

Mists arise and tree buds swell and when snow falls in spring
even in this flowerless village flowers flutter down.

9. Numbers following quotations and paraphrases from the novel refer to the page numbers in Edward Seidensticker's translation, *The Makioka Sisters,* from which all translations are taken unless otherwise indicated.
10. Tanizaki Matsuko and Edward G. Seidensticker, "Bungō o shinobu," in the supplement to Tanizaki Jun'ichirō, *Tanizaki Jun'ichirō*, 2, p. 4.
11. Tanizaki Jun'ichirō, "Sōsaku nōto: *Sasameyuki*" and "Zoku matsu no kokage."
12. Tanizaki Jun'ichirō, "Sōsaku nōto," p. 354; "Zoku matsu no kokage," p. 55.
13. Merle Rubin, Review, p. 24.
14. Ibid.
15. Noguchi, "Time," p. 28.
16. According to Ibuki Kazuko (personal interview, July 13, 1978), the writer Shiba Ryōtarō has said that he could tell from the verbosity of the narrative that Tanizaki had not witnessed the flood. The description would be more concise, according to Shiba, were it based on actual observation.
17. Paraphrased from Chiba, "*Sasameyuki* ron," p. 139. See also Kōno et al., pp. 108–109.
18. Doi Takeo, *The Anatomy of Self: The Individual Versus Society,* tr. Mark A. Harbison, p. 116.

The sisters' secrecy takes many forms. Yukiko's reticence and inarticulateness make her an enigma to people who do not know her well, and occasionally to her sisters. Sachiko is often tempted to keep things hidden from outsiders and, in the case of Taeko's affair with Itakura, even from her husband and Yukiko. Taeko tries to prevent her sisters from learning anything about her relationships with men and is not above playing her men off against each other. In fact, Taeko is surrounded by secrecy: her sisters have only a vague idea how she spends her time; when she has dysentery, she stays secretly at Kei-boy's house, where Oharu pays secret visits; Dr. Kambara secretly admits her to his hospital; and she is secreted off to a hot spring, under a false name, to have her baby—whose existence has been kept secret from almost everyone. Outsiders try to penetrate the sisters' secrets, as when a newspaper prints a distorted report of Taeko's affair with Kei-boy, and when potential marriage partners for Yukiko hire detectives to investigate the family. The Makiokas, of course, hire their own investigators and learn from them, for example, that Segoshi's mother is mentally ill.

19. Tanizaki Jun'ichirō, *Childhood Years,* p. 61.
20. Tanizaki Jun'ichirō, *The Secret History of the Lord of Musashi and Arrowroot,* pp. 109–110.
21. Tanizaki Jun'ichirō, *Naomi,* p. 55.
22. Ibid., p. 15.

23. Nakamura Shin'ichirō, p. 57. The phrase "alternative Japan," quoted below, appears in Ibid., p. 58.
24. A *waka* that Tanizaki wrote in August, 1962, reads:

> Furusato wa inakasamurai ni arasarete
> mukashi no Edo no omokage mo nashi
>
> My hometown: by rustic samurai laid waste,
> and of old Edo not a trace remains.
>
> *Tanizaki Jun'ichirō kashū,* p. 348.

25. Yoshida Seiichi, "*Sasameyuki,*" p. 185.
26. The poet and scholar Origuchi Shinobu (1887–1953) wrote of *The Makioka Sisters:* "The author has earned our gratitude, for the fact that at least this much was written down means that the fair dreams of the middle class, now in the process of disintegration, have been preserved for posterity." ("*Sasameyuki* no onna," p. 55. The translation is by Ken Ito, in *Visions of Desire,* p. 192.)
27. Mrs. Tanizaki acknowledged (in a personal interview, December 30, 1987) that she herself was the author of this and all the other *waka* in *The Makioka Sisters.* I am indebted to Chiba's "*Sasameyuki* ron" for drawing my attention to this poem. Tanizaki appears to have attached special significance to it. He chose it as his flyleaf inscription for at least one gift copy of the novel. It is also significant that he planned to cease serialization of *The Makioka Sisters* in June 1943 with the chapter that concludes with this poem. For all he knew in the spring of 1943, chapter 19 might have been the last to see print, and this poem might have marked the end of the novel. Even under the best circumstances, it would have been the last passage his readers would see until the end of the war.

7. CAPTAIN SHIGEMOTO'S MOTHER

1. Masamune Hakuchō, "Kaisetsu," pp. 201, 205. In the same essay Hakuchō writes, "If skillfully translated, *Shigemoto's Mother* might well be read with interest by Europeans and Americans [unlike translations of Jane Austen in Japan and of Tokuda Shūsei in the West, he notes], in the same way that the English translation of *The Tale of Genji* is read" (p. 206).
2. Kamei Katsuichirō, "*Shōshō Shigemoto no haha* oboegaki," p. 90. The translation is by Edward Seidensticker, in "Tanizaki Jun-ichirō, 1886–1965," p. 254.
3. Nomura, *Tanizaki Jun'ichirō: fūdo to bungaku,* p. 160.
4. The early works include the plays *Shinzei* (1911), *Hōjōji monogatari*

(The Tale of Hōjōji, 1915), and *Uguisuhime* (Princess Nightingale, 1917), and the stories "Kyōdai" (Brothers) and "Futari no chigo" (Two Acolytes), both 1918.

5. *Heichū monogatari* has been translated by Susan Downing Videen, along with a number of other premodern references to Heichū and Akutagawa's 1921 story "Kōshoku" (The Art of Love), in her *Tales of Heichū*. She discusses *Captain Shigemoto's Mother* on pp. 180–185.

6. Satō Haruo, "Saikin no Tanizaki Jun'ichirō o ronzu" (1934), in *Satō Haruo zenshū*, 11:462.

7. The depth of his interest in the Heian period and its literature is also reflected in two essays on Heian subjects that he originally planned to develop as novels, and in *The Bridge of Dreams*. The two Heian subjects are "Chino monogatari: Gansan Daishi no haha" (A Tale of Chino: Gansan Daishi's Mother, 1950) and "Ono no Takamura imōto ni koisuru koto" (Ono no Takamura Falls in Love with his Younger Sister, 1950).

8. The translation is by Makoto Ueda, in his *Modern Japanese Writers and the Nature of Literature*, p. 59.

9. This has been established by a number of commentators, including Fukui Yūko ("*Shōshō Shigemoto no haha* to koten," p. 69) and Ikeda Tsutomu ("*Shōshō Shigemoto no haha* no tenkyo ni tsuite," p. 38). The fact that the only surviving manuscript of *Tales of Heichū* had been discovered as recently as 1931 lent plausibility to the narrator's claim that he had seen a Heian manuscript that no one else knew of.

10. *Konjaku monogatarishū* 30:1, about Jijū, has been translated by Susan Downing Videen in *Tales of Heichū*, pp. 132–138.

11. The numbers following references to and quotations from the text of *Captain Shigemoto's Mother* refer to the page numbers in Tanizaki Jun'ichirō, *The Reed Cutter and Captain Shigemoto's Mother*, tr. Anthony H. Chambers.

12. The *Chokusen sakusha burui*, originally compiled in the fourteenth century, gives the lineage, rank, and dates of each known contributor to the imperial anthologies. Shigemoto appears on p. 63 of the corrected and expanded edition published by Kokugakuin in 1902. Tanizaki cites two other biographical sources on Shigemoto (*Sonpi bunmyaku* and *Kugyō bunin*), but not this one.

13. For information in this paragraph, I am indebted to Mikame Tatsuji, *Kindai bungaku no tenkyo: Kyōka to Jun'ichirō*, pp. 196–201. It is not certain even that Shigemoto was Kunitsune's son. The Muromachi genealogy *Sonpi bunmyaku* does not make it clear whether Kunitsune was Shigemoto's father or brother. See Maekawa Seitarō, "Shōshō Shigemoto no haha," p. 83.

14. *Konjaku monogatarishū* 22:8 has been translated by Marian Ury as "How

Great Minister Tokihira [Shihei] Got Major Counselor Kunitsune's Wife" in *Tales of Times Now Past*, pp. 134–138, and by Susan Downing Videen in *Tales of Heichū*, pp. 128–132.

15. In *Ishōan no yume*, pp. 212–213, Tanizaki Matsuko recalls that her husband, being seventeen years her senior, felt sorry for her and told her with tears in his eyes that he would not object to her having an affair with a younger man. He was writing *Captain Shigemoto's Mother* when he said so the first time, she says, and spoke this way only when he was in the room where he did his writing.
16. 2:449. The translation is by Paul Francis McCarthy, in "The Early Life and Works of Tanizaki Jun'ichirō," p. 145. McCarthy's discussion of *Jōtarō* and *Quicksand* has deepened my understanding of this theme.
17. Tanizaki Jun'ichirō, *The Key*, tr. Howard Hibbett, p. 93. After she has seen Kimura in the nude and he is no longer a fantasy, she retracts her observation (p. 104). Tanizaki outlined *The Key* in 1949, the same year he wrote *Captain Shigemoto's Mother*, though he did not complete *The Key* until 1956.
18. Tanizaki Jun'ichirō, *Diary of a Mad Old Man*, pp. 18, 58.
19. "Chin yeh ssu," in *Ch'uan T'ang shih*, chüan 165.
20. The man in the reeds (in *The Reed Cutter*) sings the same poem as he recalls the past. See Chapter Four, note 28.
21. Tanizaki Jun'ichirō, *The Secret History of the Lord of Musashi and Arrowroot*, p. 37.
22. Ibid., p. 31.
23. Fukui, p. 69.
24. Ury, *Tales of Times Now Past*, p. 135.
25. 13:548, my translation. Howard Hibbett's translation of the passage is on p. 75 of "A Portrait of Shunkin," in Tanizaki Jun'ichirō, *Seven Japanese Tales*.

8. THE BRIDGE OF DREAMS

1. Ibuki Kazuko, personal interview, July 13, 1993. The full translation of the title is "The Floating Bridge of Dreams," as Edward Seidensticker has called the last chapter of *The Tale of Genji*. Howard Hibbett's translation of the Tanizaki novella is entitled "The Bridge of Dreams," after Arthur Waley's *Genji*. I use Hibbett's title here for consistency. Numbers following quotations from "The Bridge of Dreams" refer to the page numbers in Hibbett's translation, in Tanizaki Jun'ichirō, *Seven Japanese Tales*, pp. 95–159.
2. Tanizaki's comment to visitors and Ibuki's conversation with Tanizaki are reported by Ibuki Kazuko in a personal letter of April 18, 1974.
3. According to Ibuki Kazuko (in her letter of April 18, 1974), the descrip-

tion of Tadasu's home matches in every detail Tanizaki's Shimogamo estate, Senkantei, where he lived from 1949 to 1956.

4. The Chinese inscription at Tanizaki's estate was different. It might be translated:

> Countless bamboo stalks detain last night's rain.
> The little path traps a fresh breeze.

5. The *yamabuki* (Kerria japonica, here translated at "double globeflowers") is associated with Mother at the climax of *Captain Shigemoto's Mother*, as well.
6. Seidensticker, *This Country, Japan*, pp. 2–3.
7. 18:199. Hibbett (p. 148) translates, "Because our house seemed so lonely and quiet," but it seems more natural to read *sabishii* (lonely) as modifying *haha* (Mother).
8. The translation is Howard Hibbett's, in Tanizaki Jun'ichirō, *Seven Japanese Tales*, pp. 183–184. The emphasis appears in the original (7:340–341), though not in Hibbett's translation.
9. Tanizaki Jun'ichirō, "Postscript," p. 466.
10. The traditional dates for the beginning and end of autumn are August 8 and November 7.
11. 18:160, my translation. Hibbett's translation of the passage is on his p. 109.
12. The name of the cottage where they meet, "Gōkantei," connotes more than the "Silk-Tree Pavilion" of the translation. *Gōkanboku* is "silk-tree"; *gōkan* alone means "taking pleasure together," particularly pleasure between a man and a woman.
13. 18:187; Hibbett translation, p. 135. "Beget" [*mōkete*] replaces Hibbett's "have."
14. Though *The Bridge of Dreams* remains ambiguous, there is clear external evidence that Tanizaki intended a sexual relationship between Tadasu and his stepmother. In his review of Minakami Tsutomu's *Echizen takeningyō* (The Bamboo Doll of Echizen, 1963), Tanizaki writes:

> In *The Bridge of Dreams*, Tadasu takes his stepmother Tsuneko as his *de facto* wife on his father's instructions; but in *The Bamboo Doll*, Kisuke loves Tamae as if she were his real mother and refuses to take her as his wife, even though they live together. Tamae nevertheless wants to be loved by Kisuke as she has been by his father, and hopes that one day he will embrace her. In feeling, the story resembles *The Bridge of Dreams*.
>
> (22:520)

In a personal letter of May 25, 1987, Ibuki Kazuko recalls Tanizaki telling her that, as far as he was concerned, there was an incestuous relationship between Tadasu and his stepmother ("boshisōkan wa atta koto ni shite iru tsumori da").

15. Haruo Shirane summarizes the various interpretations of the title "Yume no ukihashi" in the *Genji* in *The Bridge of Dreams: A Poetics of* The Tale of Genji, pp. 192–193.
16. On allusive variation (*honkadori*), see Chapter Four, page 37.
17. Murasaki, p. 16.
18. One critic who indicts Sawako is Hino Keizō, in "Haha naru mono: *Yume no ukihashi* ron," p. 309. She is the culprit in a 1990 television adaptation, as well. It was one of my students, Janet Klein, who first suggested to me that Tadasu might be involved.
19. Murasaki, p. 92.
20. Shigemoto, too, takes a special interest in his younger half-brother Atsutada, because he resembles their mother (16:271); Jun'ichirō Tanizaki, *The Reed Cutter and Captain Shigemoto's Mother*, p. 169.
21. Hata Kōhei makes some of the same points about the relationship of *The Bridge of Dreams* to the *Genji* and reaches some of the same conclusions–that Takeshi is Tadasu's son and that Tadasu will live with him as both parent and lover; but Hata bases his analysis more on *Genji* parallels that he finds in Tanizaki's personal life than on internal evidence. See Hata, *Tanizaki Jun'ichirō:* Genji monogatari *taiken*, pp. 5–74.
22. Murasaki, p. 48.
23. This interpretation is plausible and possible, and that is the point. There is no proof: like Tsuneko's death–like so many of Tanizaki's narratives–Tadasu's relationship with Takeshi is suggestive and equivocal. Each reader will make of it what he or she may.

List of Works Cited

(All items in Japanese are published in Tokyo unless otherwise indicated.)

Ara Masahito, ed. *Tanizaki Jun'ichirō kenkyū.* Kindai bungaku kenkyū sōsho. Yagi Shoten, 1972.

Brower, Robert H. and Earl Miner. *Japanese Court Poetry.* Stanford, Stanford University Press, 1961.

Brownlee, John, tr. "Jikkinshō," *Monumenta Nipponica* 29.2:141–142 (Summer 1974).

Chiba Shunji. "'Aozuka-shi no hanashi' ni tsuite: Taishō kara Shōwa e no Tanizaki Jun'ichirō," *Nihon kindai bungaku* 23:149–161 (October 1976). Reprinted as "Taishō kara Shōwa e no Tanizaki Jun'ichirō: 'Aozuka-shi no hanashi' wo chūshin ni," in Chiba Shunji, ed., *Tanizaki Jun'ichirō: monogatari no hōhō,* pp. 115–127. Nihon bungaku kenkyū shiryō shinshū. Yūseidō, 1990.

——. "Tanizaki Jun'ichirō *Bushūkō hiwa* ni tsuite," *Nihon kindai bungaku* 28:197–210 (September 1981).

——. "*Sasameyuki* ron," *Kokubungaku kaishaku to kanshō* 52.4:131–144 (April 1987).

——. "Katari no nawa—Hata Kōhei 'Shunkin jigai' wo bakusu," *Dokusha* 4:2–9 (Summer 1989).

——, ed. *Tanizaki Jun'ichirō.* Kanshō Nihon gendai bungaku. Kadokawa Shoten, 1982.

——, ed. *Tanizaki Jun'ichirō: monogatari no hōhō.* Nihon bungaku kenkyū shiryō shinshū. Yūseidō, 1990.

Chokusen sakusha burui. Kokugakuin, 1902.

Doi Takeo. *The Anatomy of Self: The Individual Versus Society,* tr. Mark A. Harbison. Tokyo, Kodansha International, 1986.

Fukuda Kiyoto and Hirayama Jōji. *Tanizaki Jun'ichirō: hito to sakuhin.* Shimizu Shoin, 1969.

Fukui Yūko. "*Shōshō Shigemoto no haha* to koten," *Rikkyō Daigaku Nihon bungaku* 20:66–74 (June 1968).

Gerstle, C. Andrew, Kiyoshi Inobe, and William P. Malm. *Theater as Music: The Bunraku Play "Mt. Imo and Mt. Se: An Exemplary Tale of Womanly Virtue."* Ann Arbor, Center for Japanese Studies, The University of Michigan, 1990.

Hardy, Thomas. *A Group of Noble Dames.* New York and London, Harper and Bros., 1891.

Hashimoto Yoshiichirō. *Tanizaki Jun'ichirō no bungaku,* rev. ed. Ōfūsha, 1976.

Hata Kōhei. "Oyūsama: waga Tanizaki no *Ashikari* kō," *Umi,* July 1976, pp. 220–240.

———. *Tanizaki Jun'ichirō:* Genji monogatari *taiken.* Chikuma Shobō, 1976.

———. *Kami to gangu to no aida: Shōwa shonen no Tanizaki Jun'ichirō.* Rokkō Shuppan, 1977.

———. *Tanizaki Jun'ichirō.* Chikuma Shobō, 1989.

Hino Keizō. "Haha naru mono: *Yume no ukihashi* ron," in Ara Masahito, ed., *Tanizaki Jun'ichirō kenkyū,* pp. 309–310. Kindai bungaku kenkyū sōsho. Yagi Shoten, 1972.

Ibuki Kazuko. Personal letters of December 7, 1973; April 18, 1974; and May 25, 1987; and personal interviews.

Ikeda Tsutomu. "*Shōshō Shigemoto no haha* no tenkyo ni tsuite," *Kokubungaku: kaishaku to kanshō* 32:35–44 (March 1967).

Inazawa Hideo. *Tanizaki Jun'ichirō no sekai.* Shichōsha, 1979.

Ito, Ken. *Visions of Desire: Tanizaki's Fictional Worlds,* Stanford, Stanford University Press, 1991.

Itō Sei. "Kaisetsu," in Tanizaki Jun'ichirō, *Bushūkō hiwa.* Shinchō Bunko, 1953, pp. 182–184.

———. *Tanizaki Jun'ichirō no bungaku.* Chūō Kōronsha, 1970.

Kamei Katsuichirō. "*Shōshō Shigemoto no haha* oboegaki," *Bungei,* May 1956, pp. 87–90.

Katō, Eileen, tr. "Kinuta," *Monumenta Nipponica* 32.3:332–346 (Autumn 1977).

Kazamaki Keijirō and Yoshida Seiichi, eds. *Tanizaki Jun'ichirō no bungaku.* Hanawa Shobō, 1954.

Keene, Donald. "Kaisetsu," in *Tanizaki Jun'ichirō,* 3, pp. 542–560. Nihon no bungaku. Chūō Kōronsha, 1967.

———. *Dawn to the West: Japanese Literature in the Modern Era: Fiction.* New York, Holt, Rinehart and Winston, 1984.

———, ed. *Twenty Plays of the Nō Theatre.* New York, Columbia University Press, 1970.

Kobayashi, Hiroko. *The Human Comedy of Heian Japan: A Study of the Secular Stories in the Twelfth-Century Collection of Tales, Konjaku Monogatari-shū.* Tokyo, Centre for East Asian Cultural Studies, 1979.

Kōno Taeko. *Tanizaki bungaku to kōtei no yokubō.* Bungei Shunjū, 1976.

Kōno Toshirō, ed. *Ronkō Tanizaki Jun'ichirō.* Ōfūsha, 1980.

———, Chiba Shunji, et al. "Tanizaki no sakuhin o yominaosu," *Kokubungaku kaishaku to kyōzai no kenkyū* 30.9:88–117 (August 1985).

LaFleur, William R. *The Karma of Words: Buddhism and the Literary Arts in Medieval Japan.* Berkeley, University of California Press, 1983.

Liman, Anthony V. "The True Mark of a Saint: Robertson Davies' *Fifth Business* and Jun'ichirō Tanizaki's *A Portrait of Shunkin,*" in Kinya Tsuruta and Theodore Goossen, eds., *Nature and Identity in Canadian and Japanese Literature,* pp. 87–108. Toronto, University of Toronto/York University Joint Centre for Asia Pacific Studies, 1988.

Maeda Hisanori. "Monogatari no kōzō: Tanizaki Jun'ichirō *Shunkinshō,*" *Kokubungaku kaishaku to kyōzai no kenkyū* 34.8:95–101 (July 1989).

Maekawa Seitarō. "Shōshō Shigemoto no haha," *Nihon kindai bungaku* 21:74–89 (1974).

Marra, Michele. "The Buddhist Mythmaking of Defilement: Sacred Courtesans in Medieval Japan," *The Journal of Asian Studies* 52.1:49–65 (February 1993).

Masamune Hakuchō. "Kaisetsu," in Tanizaki Jun'ichirō, *Shōshō Shigemoto no haha.* Kadokawa Bunko, 1953, pp. 201–209.

———. "*Shunkinshō* sono ta," *Bungei, Tanizaki Jun'ichirō tokuhon,* May 30, 1956, pp. 81–82.

———. "*Bushūkō hiwa* atogaki," in *Masamune Hakuchō zenshū,* 6:363–365. Shinchōsha, 1965.

———. *Masamune Hakuchō zenshū,* 13 vols. Shinchōsha, 1965–1968.

McCarthy, Paul Francis. "The Early Life and Works of Tanizaki Jun'ichirō." Ph.D. dissertation, Harvard University, 1975.

Mikame Tatsuji. "Tanizaki no *Ashikari* ni okeru nōgakuteki kōsei," *Kokugo kokubun kaishaku,* July 1973, pp. 40–49. (Reprinted, with revisions, in his *Kindai bungaku no tenkyo: Kyōka to Jun'ichirō,* pp. 141–161.)

———. *Kindai bungaku no tenkyo: Kyōka to Jun'ichirō.* Sasama Shoin, 1974.

Minakami Tsutomu. "Tanizaki sensei no shokan: aru shuppansha shachō e no tegami o yomu, sono ni," *Chūō kōron bungei tokushū,* March 25, 1985, pp. 205–215.

Miner, Earl, Hiroko Odagiri, and Robert E. Morrell. *The Princeton Companion to Classical Japanese Literature.* Princeton, Princeton University Press, 1985.

Miyauchi Junko. "Tanizaki Jun'ichirō *Ashikari Yume no ukihashi* nado," in Chiba Shunji, ed., *Tanizaki Jun'ichirō: monogatari no hōhō,* pp. 150–157. Nihon bungaku kenkyū shiryō shinshū. Yūseidō, 1990.

Mueller, Jacqueline, tr. "The Two Shizukas," *Monumenta Nipponica* 36.3:285–298 (Autumn 1981).

Murasaki Shikibu. *The Tale of Genji,* tr. Edward G. Seidensticker. New York, Knopf, 1976.

Nagae Hironobu. *Tanizaki Jun'ichirō shiron: bosei e no shiten.* Shin'ei kenkyū sōshō. Yūseidō, 1988.

Nakamura Shin'ichirō. "Tanizaki to *Sasameyuki,*" in *Tanizaki Jun'ichirō,* pp. 56–64. Nihon bungaku kenkyū shiryō sōsho. Yūseidō, 1972.

Nippon Gakujutsu Shinkōkai. *Japanese Noh Drama,* 3 vols. Tokyo, 1955–1960.

Noda Yoshio. "Mōmoku monogatari, Shunkinshō," in Kazamaki Keijirō and Yoshida Seiichi, eds., *Tanizaki Jun'ichirō no bungaku,* pp. 241–260. Hanawa Shobō, 1954.

Noguchi Takehiko. *Tanizaki Jun'ichirō ron.* Chūō Kōronsha, 1973.

——. "Time in the World of *Sasameyuki* [The Makioka Sisters]," tr. Teruko Craig, *The Journal of Japanese Studies* 3.1:1–36 (Winter 1977). (A translation of Chapter Six of Noguchi's *Tanizaki Jun'ichirō ron.*)

Nomura Shōgo. *Tanizaki Jun'ichirō: fūdo to bungaku.* Chūō Kōronsha, 1973.

——. *Denki Tanizaki Jun'ichirō,* revised edition. Rokkō Shuppan, 1974.

——. *Tanizaki Jun'ichirō no sakuhin.* Rokkō Shuppan, 1974.

Nosaka Akiyuki. "Shunkinshō," *Kokubungaku kaishaku to kyōzai no kenkyū* 23.10:90–91 (August 1978).

Origuchi Shinobu. "*Sasameyuki* no onna," in *Tanizaki Jun'ichirō,* pp. 49–55. Nihon bungaku kenkyū shiryō sōsho. Yūseidō, 1972.

Ōhashi Takahiko. "*Yoshino kuzu* no sekai," in Kōno Toshirō, ed., *Ronkō Tanizaki Jun'ichirō,* pp. 197–213. Ōfūsha, 1980.

Ōoka Shōhei. "*Shunkinshō kōgo* no tokugokan," *Tanizaki Jun'ichirō,* pp. 250–252. Nihon bungaku kenkyū shiryō sōsho. Yūseidō, 1972.

Ōta Saburō. "Thomas Hardy to Tanizaki Jun'ichirō: *Shunkinshō* o meguru mondai," in *Tanizaki Jun'ichirō,* pp. 143–157. Nihon bungaku kenkyū shiryō sōsho. Yūseidō, 1972.

Rimer, J. Thomas. *Modern Japanese Fiction and Its Traditions: An Introduction.* Princeton, Princeton University Press, 1978.

Rubin, Jay. *Injurious to Public Morals: Writers and the Meiji State.* Seattle, University of Washington Press, 1984.

Rubin, Merle. Review of Robert Kee, *1939: In the Shadow of War. Christian Science Monitor,* June 7, 1984, p. 24.

Saeki Junko. *Yūjo no bunka shi.* Chūō Kōronsha, 1987.

Satō Haruo. *Satō Haruo zenshū,* 12 vols. Kōdansha, 1966–1970.

——. "Saikin no Tanizaki Jun'ichirō o ronzu," in *Satō Haruo zenshū,* 11:462. Kōdansha, 1969.

Schnitzler, Arthur. *The Shepherd's Pipe and Other Stories,* tr. O. F. Theis. Freeport, N.Y., Books For Libraries Press, 1970 (reprint of 1922 edition).

Seidensticker, Edward. "Tanizaki Jun-ichirō, 1886–1965," *Monumenta Nipponica* 21:249–265 (1966).

——. *This Country, Japan.* Tokyo, Kodansha International, 1979.

——. *Tokyo Rising: The City Since the Great Earthquake.* New York, Knopf, 1990.

Shirane, Haruo. *The Bridge of Dreams: A Poetics of "The Tale of Genji."* Stanford, Stanford University Press, 1987.

Sugimori Hisahide. "Shunkinshō," in Ara Masahito, ed., *Tanizaki Jun'ichirō kenkyū,* pp. 187–191. Kindai bungaku kenkyū sōsho. Yagi Shoten, 1972.

Tahara, Mildred M., tr. *Tales of Yamato: A Tenth-Century Poem-Tale.* Honolulu, University Press of Hawaii, 1980.

Takakuwa Noriko. "*Yoshino kuzu* ron: gengoteki hokōsha no katari to shite," in Chiba Shunji, ed., *Tanizaki Jun'ichirō: monogatari no hōhō,* pp. 140–149. Nihon bungaku kenkyū shiryō shinshū. Yūseidō, 1990.

Takeuchi Kiyomi. "Tanizaki Jun'ichirō *Ashikari* ron: sono kokubungakuteki kōzō," *Geijutsu shijōshugi bungei* 3:51–58 (September 1977).

Tanizaki Jun'ichirō. "The White Fox," tr. Eric S. Bell and Eiji Ukai. *Eminent Authors of Contemporary Japan,* vol. 1, pp. 1–37. Tokyo, Kaitakusha, 1930.

—— [Tanizaki Jun-ichiro]. *Ashikari and the Story of Shunkin,* tr. Roy Humpherson and Hajime Okita. Hokuseidō, 1936; reprinted by Greenwood Press, Westport, Conn., 1970.

—— [Tanizaki Junichiro]. *Some Prefer Nettles,* tr. Edward G. Seidensticker. New York, Knopf, 1955.

—— [Tanizaki Junichirō]. *The Makioka Sisters,* tr. Edward G. Seidensticker. New York, Knopf, 1957.

—— [Tanizaki Junichiro]. *The Key,* tr. Howard Hibbett. New York, Knopf, 1961.

—— [Tanizaki Junichiro]. *Seven Japanese Tales,* tr. Howard Hibbett. New York, Knopf, 1963. Contains "A Portrait of Shunkin," "Terror," "The Bridge of Dreams," "The Tatooer," "The Thief," "Aguri," and "A Blind Man's Tale."

—— [Tanizaki Junichiro]. *Diary of a Mad Old Man,* tr. Howard Hibbett. New York, Knopf, 1965.

——. *Tanizaki Jun'ichirō,* 3 vols. Nihon no bungaku. Chūō Kōronsha, 1966–1967.

——. *Tanizaki Jun'ichirō zenshū,* 28 vols. Chūō Kōronsha, 1966–1968.

——. "Sōsaku nōto: *Sasameyuki,*" *Chūō kōron* 85.12:352–364 (December 1970).

——. *Tanizaki Jun'ichirō kashū.* Osaka, Yukawa Shobō, 1977.

——. *In Praise of Shadows,* tr. Thomas J. Harper and Edward G. Seidensticker. New Haven, Conn., Leete's Island Books, 1977.

——. "Longing for Mother," tr. Edward Fowler, *Monumenta Nipponica* 35.4:467–483 (Winter 1980).

——. "Postscript to 'A Portrait of Shunkin,'" tr. Anthony H. Chambers, *Monumenta Nipponica* 35.4:457–466 (Winter 1980).

—— [Tanizaki Junichirō]. *The Secret History of the Lord of Musashi and Arrowroot,* tr. Anthony H. Chambers. New York, Knopf, 1982.

——. "Zoku matsu no kokage," *Chūō kōron bungei tokushū,* October, 1984, pp. 43–71.

—— [Tanizaki Junichirō]. *Naomi,* tr. Anthony H. Chambers. New York, Knopf, 1985.

—— [Tanizaki Jun'ichiro]. *Childhood Years: A Memoir,* tr. Paul McCarthy. Tokyo, Kodansha International, 1988.

—— [Tanizaki Jun'ichiro]. *A Cat, A Man, and Two Women,* tr. Paul McCarthy. Tokyo, Kodansha International, 1990. Also contains "The Little Kingdom" and "Professor Rado."

—— [Tanizaki Junichirō]. *Quicksand,* tr. Howard Hibbett. New York, Knopf, 1994.

—— [Tanizaki Junichirō]. *The Reed Cutter and Captain Shigemoto's Mother: Two Novellas,* tr. Anthony H. Chambers. New York, Knopf, 1994.

Tanizaki Matsuko. *Ishōan no yume.* Chūō Kōronsha, 1967.

—— and Edward G. Seidensticker. "Bungō o shinobu." In the supplement to Tanizaki Jun'ichirō, *Tanizaki Jun'ichirō,* 2, pp. 1–9. Nihon no bungaku. Chūō Kōronsha, 1966.

Tyler, Royall, tr. *Pining Wind: A Cycle of Nō Plays.* Cornell University East Asia Papers. Ithaca, 1978.

——, tr. *Granny Mountains: A Second Cycle of Nō Plays.* Cornell University East Asia Papers. Ithaca, 1978.

Ueda Akinari. *Ugetsu Monogatari: Tales of Moonlight and Rain,* tr. Leon Zolbrod. Vancouver, University of British Columbia Press, 1974.

Ueda, Makoto. *Modern Japanese Writers and the Nature of Literature.* Stanford, Stanford University Press, 1976.

Ury, Marian, tr. *Tales of Times Now Past: Sixty-Two Stories from a Medieval Japanese Collection.* Berkeley, University of California Press, 1979.

Videen, Susan Downing. *Tales of Heichū.* Harvard East Asian Monographs, 137. Cambridge, Council on East Asian Studies, Harvard University, 1989.

Yabe Ryōsaku. "*Shunkinshō* zengo no omoide," *Geppō* 16, p. 5 (February 1968). *Tanizaki Jun'ichirō zenshū.* Chūō Kōronsha, 1966–1968.

Yokomichi Mario and Omote Akira, eds. *Yōkyokushū* I. Nihon koten bungaku taikei. Iwanami, 1960.

Yoshida Seiichi. "*Sasameyuki,*" in Yoshida Seiichi, ed., *Tanizaki Jun'ichirō,* pp. 165–188. Kindai bunkagu kanshō kōza. Kadokawa Shoten, 1959.

——, ed. *Tanizaki Jun'ichirō.* Kindai bunkagu kanshō kōza. Kadokawa Shoten, 1959.

Index

Harvard East Asian Monographs

1. Liang Fang-chung, *The Single-Whip Method of Taxation in China*
2. Harold C. Hinton, *The Grain Tribute System of China, 1845–1911*
3. Ellsworth C. Carlson, *The Kaiping Mines, 1877–1912*
4. Chao Kuo-chün, *Agrarian Policies of Mainland China: A Documentary Study, 1949–1956*
5. Edgar Snow, *Random Notes on Red China, 1936–1945*
6. Edwin George Beal, Jr., *The Origin of Likin, 1835–1864*
7. Chao Kuo-chün, *Economic Planning and Organization in Mainland China: A Documentary Study, 1949–1957*
8. John K. Fairbank, *Ch'ing Documents: An Introductory Syllabus*
9. Helen Yin and Yi-chang Yin, *Economic Statistics of Mainland China, 1949–1957*
10. Wolfgang Franke, *The Reform and Abolition of the Traditional Chinese Examination System*
11. Albert Feuerwerker and S. Cheng, *Chinese Communist Studies of Modern Chinese History*
12. C. John Stanley, *Late Ch'ing Finance: Hu Kuang-yung as an Innovator*
13. S. M. Meng, *The Tsungli Yamen: Its Organization and Functions*
14. Ssu-yü Teng, *Historiography of the Taiping Rebellion*
15. Chun-Jo Liu, *Controversies in Modern Chinese Intellectual History: An Analytic Bibliography of Periodical Articles, Mainly of the May Fourth and Post-May Fourth Era*
16. Edward J. M. Rhoads, *The Chinese Red Army, 1927–1963: An Annotated Bibliography*
17. Andrew J. Nathan, *A History of the China International Famine Relief Commission*
18. Frank H. H. King (ed.) and Prescott Clarke, *A Research Guide to China-Coast Newspapers, 1822–1911*
19. Ellis Joffe, *Party and Army: Professionalism and Political Control in the Chinese Officer Corps, 1949–1964*

20. Toshio G. Tsukahira, *Feudal Control in Tokugawa Japan: The Sankin Kōtai System*
21. Kwang-Ching Liu, ed., *American Missionaries in China: Papers from Harvard Seminars*
22. George Moseley, *A Sino-Soviet Cultural Frontier: The Ili Kazakh Autonomous Chou*
23. Carl F. Nathan, *Plague Prevention and Politics in Manchuria, 1910–1931*
24. Adrian Arthur Bennett, *John Fryer: The Introduction of Western Science and Technology into Nineteenth-Century China*
25. Donald J. Friedman, *The Road from Isolation: The Campaign of the American Committee for Non-Participation in Japanese Aggression, 1938–1941*
26. Edward LeFevour, *Western Enterprise in Late Ch'ing China: A Selective Survey of Jardine, Matheson and Company's Operations, 1842–1895*
27. Charles Neuhauser, *Third World Politics: China and the Afro-Asian People's Solidarity Organization, 1957–1967*
28. Kungtu C. Sun, assisted by Ralph W. Huenemann, *The Economic Development of Manchuria in the First Half of the Twentieth Century*
29. Shahid Javed Burki, *A Study of Chinese Communes, 1965*
30. John Carter Vincent, *The Extraterritorial System in China: Final Phase*
31. Madeleine Chi, *China Diplomacy, 1914–1918*
32. Clifton Jackson Phillips, *Protestant America and the Pagan World: The First Half Century of the American Board of Commissioners for Foreign Missions, 1810–1860*
33. James Pusey, *Wu Han: Attacking the Present through the Past*
34. Ying-wan Cheng, *Postal Communication in China and Its Modernization, 1860–1896*
35. Tuvia Blumenthal, *Saving in Postwar Japan*
36. Peter Frost, *The Bakumatsu Currency Crisis*
37. Stephen C. Lockwood, *Augustine Heard and Company, 1858–1862*
38. Robert R. Campbell, *James Duncan Campbell: A Memoir by His Son*
39. Jerome Alan Cohen, ed., *The Dynamics of China's Foreign Relations*
40. V. V. Vishnyakova-Akimova, *Two Years in Revolutionary China, 1925–1927*, tr. Steven I. Levine
41. Meron Medzini, *French Policy in Japan during the Closing Years of the Tokugawa Regime*
42. *The Cultural Revolution in the Provinces*
43. Sidney A. Forsythe, *An American Missionary Community in China, 1895–1905*
44. Benjamin I. Schwartz, ed., *Reflections on the May Fourth Movement: A Symposium*
45. Ching Young Choe, *The Rule of the Taewŏn'gun, 1864–1873: Restoration in Yi Korea*

46. W. P. J. Hall, *A Bibliographical Guide to Japanese Research on the Chinese Economy, 1958–1970*
47. Jack J. Gerson, *Horatio Nelson Lay and Sino-British Relations, 1854–1864*
48. Paul Richard Bohr, *Famine and the Missionary: Timothy Richard as Relief Administrator and Advocate of National Reform*
49. Endymion Wilkinson, *The History of Imperial China: A Research Guide*
50. Britten Dean, *China and Great Britain: The Diplomacy of Commercial Relations, 1860–1864*
51. Ellsworth C. Carlson, *The Foochow Missionaries, 1847–1880*
52. Yeh-chien Wang, *An Estimate of the Land-Tax Collection in China, 1753 and 1908*
53. Richard M. Pfeffer, *Understanding Business Contracts in China, 1949–1963*
54. Han-sheng Chuan and Richard Kraus, *Mid-Ch'ing Rice Markets and Trade: An Essay in Price History*
55. Ranbir Vohra, *Lao She and the Chinese Revolution*
56. Liang-lin Hsiao, *China's Foreign Trade Statistics, 1864–1949*
57. Lee-hsia Hsu Ting, *Government Control of the Press in Modern China, 1900–1949*
58. Edward W. Wagner, *The Literati Purges: Political Conflict in Early Yi Korea*
59. Joungwon A. Kim, *Divided Korea: The Politics of Development, 1945–1972*
60. Noriko Kamachi, John K. Fairbank, and Chūzō Ichiko, *Japanese Studies of Modern China Since 1953: A Bibliographical Guide to Historical and Social-Science Research on the Nineteenth and Twentieth Centuries, Supplementary Volume for 1953–1969*
61. Donald A. Gibbs and Yun-chen Li, *A Bibliography of Studies and Translations of Modern Chinese Literature, 1918–1942*
62. Robert H. Silin, *Leadership and Values: The Organization of Large-Scale Taiwanese Enterprises*
63. David Pong, *A Critical Guide to the Kwangtung Provincial Archives Deposited at the Public Record Office of London*
64. Fred W. Drake, *China Charts the World: Hsu Chi-yü and His Geography of 1848*
65. William A. Brown and Urgunge Onon, translators and annotators, *History of the Mongolian People's Republic*
66. Edward L. Farmer, *Early Ming Government: The Evolution of Dual Capitals*
67. Ralph C. Croizier, *Koxinga and Chinese Nationalism: History, Myth, and the Hero*
68. William J. Tyler, tr., *The Psychological World of Natsume Sōseki*, by Doi Takeo

69. Eric Widmer, *The Russian Ecclesiastical Mission in Peking during the Eighteenth Century*
70. Charlton M. Lewis, *Prologue to the Chinese Revolution: The Transformation of Ideas and Institutions in Hunan Province, 1891–1907*
71. Preston Torbert, *The Ch'ing Imperial Household Department: A Study of its Organization and Principal Functions, 1662–1796*
72. Paul A. Cohen and John E. Schrecker, eds., *Reform in Nineteenth-Century China*
73. Jon Sigurdson, *Rural Industrialism in China*
74. Kang Chao, *The Development of Cotton Textile Production in China*
75. Valentin Rabe, *The Home Base of American China Missions, 1880–1920*
76. Sarasin Viraphol, *Tribute and Profit: Sino-Siamese Trade, 1652–1853*
77. Ch'i-ch'ing Hsiao, *The Military Establishment of the Yuan Dynasty*
78. Meishi Tsai, *Contemporary Chinese Novels and Short Stories, 1949–1974: An Annotated Bibliography*
79. Wellington K. K. Chan, *Merchants, Mandarins and Modern Enterprise in Late Ch'ing China*
80. Endymion Wilkinson, *Landlord and Labor in Late Imperial China: Case Studies from Shandong by Jing Su and Luo Lun*
81. Barry Keenan, *The Dewey Experiment in China: Educational Reform and Political Power in the Early Republic*
82. George A. Hayden, *Crime and Punishment in Medieval Chinese Drama: Three Judge Pao Plays*
83. Sang-Chul Suh, *Growth and Structural Changes in the Korean Economy, 1910–1940*
84. J. W. Dower, *Empire and Aftermath: Yoshida Shigeru and the Japanese Experience, 1878–1954*
85. Martin Collcutt, *Five Mountains: The Rinzai Zen Monastic Institution in Medieval Japan*
86. Kwang Suk Kim and Michael Roemer, *Growth and Structural Transformation*
87. Anne O. Krueger, *The Developmental Role of the Foreign Sector and Aid*
88. Edwin S. Mills and Byung-Nak Song, *Urbanization and Urban Problems*
89. Sung Hwan Ban, Pal Yong Moon, and Dwight H. Perkins, *Rural Development*
90. Noel F. McGinn, Donald R. Snodgrass, Yung Bong Kim, Shin-Bok Kim, and Quee-Young Kim, *Education and Development in Korea*
91. Leroy P. Jones and Il SaKong, *Government, Business, and Entrepreneurship in Economic Development: The Korean Case*
92. Edward S. Mason, Dwight H. Perkins, Kwang Suk Kim, David C. Cole, Mahn Je Kim, et al., *The Economic and Social Modernization of the Republic of Korea*

93. Robert Repetto, Tai Hwan Kwon, Son-Ung Kim, Dae Young Kim, John E. Sloboda, and Peter J. Donaldson, *Economic Development, Population Policy, and Demographic Transition in the Republic of Korea*
94. Parks M. Coble, Jr., *The Shanghai Capitalists and the Nationalist Government, 1927–1937*
95. Noriko Kamachi, *Reform in China: Huang Tsun-hsien and the Japanese Model*
96. Richard Wich, *Sino-Soviet Crisis Politics: A Study of Political Change and Communication*
97. Lillian M. Li, *China's Silk Trade: Traditional Industry in the Modern World, 1842–1937*
98. R. David Arkush, *Fei Xiaotong and Sociology in Revolutionary China*
99. Kenneth Alan Grossberg, *Japan's Renaissance: The Politics of the Muromachi Bakufu*
100. James Reeve Pusey, *China and Charles Darwin*
101. Hoyt Cleveland Tillman, *Utilitarian Confucianism: Ch'en Liang's Challenge to Chu Hsi*
102. Thomas A. Stanley, *Ōsugi Sakae, Anarchist in Taishō Japan: The Creativity of the Ego*
103. Jonathan K. Ocko, *Bureaucratic Reform in Provincial China: Ting Jih-ch'ang in Restoration Kiangsu, 1867–1870*
104. James Reed, *The Missionary Mind and American East Asia Policy, 1911–1915*
105. Neil L. Waters, *Japan's Local Pragmatists: The Transition from Bakumatsu to Meiji in the Kawasaki Region*
106. David C. Cole and Yung Chul Park, *Financial Development in Korea, 1945–1978*
107. Roy Bahl, Chuk Kyo Kim, and Chong Kee Park, *Public Finances during the Korean Modernization Process*
108. William D. Wray, *Mitsubishi and the N.Y.K., 1870–1914: Business Strategy in the Japanese Shipping Industry*
109. Ralph William Huenemann, *The Dragon and the Iron Horse: The Economics of Railroads in China, 1876–1937*
110. Benjamin A. Elman, *From Philosophy to Philology: Intellectual and Social Aspects of Change in Late Imperial China*
111. Jane Kate Leonard, *Wei Yuan and China's Rediscovery of the Maritime World*
112. Luke S. K. Kwong, *A Mosaic of the Hundred Days: Personalities, Politics, and Ideas of 1898*
113. John E. Wills, Jr., *Embassies and Illusions: Dutch and Portuguese Envoys to K'ang-hsi, 1666–1687*
114. Joshua A. Fogel, *Politics and Sinology: The Case of Naitō Konan (1866–1934)*

115. Jeffrey C. Kinkley, ed., *After Mao: Chinese Literature and Society, 1978–1981*
116. C. Andrew Gerstle, *Circles of Fantasy: Convention in the Plays of Chikamatsu*
117. Andrew Gordon, *The Evolution of Labor Relations in Japan: Heavy Industry, 1853–1955*
118. Daniel K. Gardner, *Chu Hsi and the* Ta Hsueh: *Neo-Confucian Reflection on the Confucian Canon*
119. Christine Guth Kanda, *Shinzō: Hachiman Imagery and its Development*
120. Robert Borgen, *Sugawara no Michizane and the Early Heian Court*
121. Chang-tai Hung, *Going to the People: Chinese Intellectual and Folk Literature, 1918–1937*
122. Michael A. Cusumano, *The Japanese Automobile Industry: Technology and Management at Nissan and Toyota*
123. Richard von Glahn, *The Country of Streams and Grottoes: Expansion, Settlement, and the Civilizing of the Sichuan Frontier in Song Times*
124. Steven D. Carter, *The Road to Komatsubara: A Classical Reading of the Renga Hyakuin*
125. Katherine F. Bruner, John K. Fairbank, and Richard T. Smith, *Entering China's Service: Robert Hart's Journals, 1854–1863*
126. Bob Tadashi Wakabayashi, *Anti-Foreignism and Western Learning in Early-Modern Japan: The* New Theses *of 1825*
127. Atsuko Hirai, *Individualism and Socialism: The Life and Thought of Kawai Eijirō (1891–1944)*
128. Ellen Widmer, *The Margins of Utopia:* Shui-hu hou-chuan *and the Literature of Ming Loyalism*
129. R. Kent Guy, *The Emperor's Four Treasuries: Scholars and the State in the Late Ch'ien-lung Era*
130. Peter C. Perdue, *Exhausting the Earth: State and Peasant in Hunan, 1500–1850*
131. Susan Chan Egan, *A Latterday Confucian: Reminiscences of William Hung (1893–1980)*
132. James T. C. Liu, *China Turning Inward: Intellectual-Political Changes in the Early Twelfth Century*
133. Paul A. Cohen, *Between Tradition and Modernity: Wang T'ao and Reform in Late Ch'ing China*
134. Kate Wildman Nakai, *Shogunal Politics: Arai Hakuseki and the Premises of Tokugawa Rule*
135. Parks M. Coble, *Facing Japan: Chinese Politics and Japanese Imperialism, 1931–1937*
136. Jon L. Saari, *Legacies of Childhood: Growing Up Chinese in a Time of Crisis, 1890–1920*
137. Susan Downing Videen, *Tales of Heichū*

138. Heinz Morioka and Miyoko Sasaki, *Rakugo: The Popular Narrative Art of Japan*
139. Joshua A. Fogel, *Nakae Ushikichi in China: The Mourning of Spirit*
140. Alexander Barton Woodside, *Vietnam and the Chinese Model: A Comparative Study of Vietnamese and Chinese Government in the First Half of the Nineteenth Century*
141. George Elison, *Deus Destroyed: The Image of Christianity in Early Modern Japan*
142. William D. Wray, ed., *Managing Industrial Enterprise: Cases from Japan's Prewar Experience*
143. T'ung-tsu Ch'ü, *Local Government in China under the Ch'ing*
144. Marie Anchordoguy, *Computers, Inc.: Japan's Challenge to IBM*
145. Barbara Molony, *Technology and Investment: The Prewar Japanese Chemical Industry*
146. Mary Elizabeth Berry, *Hideyoshi*
147. Laura E. Hein, *Fueling Growth: The Energy Revolution and Economic Policy in Postwar Japan*
148. Wen-hsin Yeh, *The Alienated Academy: Culture and Politics in Republican China, 1919–1937*
149. Dru C. Gladney, *Muslim Chinese: Ethnic Nationalism in the People's Republic*
150. Merle Goldman and Paul A. Cohen, eds., *Ideas Across Cultures: Essays on Chinese Thought in Honor of Benjamin I. Schwartz*
151. James Polachek, *The Inner Opium War*
152. Gail Lee Bernstein, *Japanese Marxist: A Portrait of Kawakami Hajime, 1879–1946*
153. Lloyd E. Eastman, *The Abortive Revolution: China under Nationalist Rule, 1927–1937*
154. Mark Mason, *American Multinationals and Japan: The Political Economy of Japanese Capital Controls, 1899–1980*
155. Richard J. Smith, John K. Fairbank, and Katherine F. Bruner, *Robert Hart and China's Early Modernization: His Journals, 1863–1866*
156. George J. Tanabe, Jr., *Myōe the Dreamkeeper: Fantasy and Knowledge in Kamakura Buddhism*
157. William Wayne Farris, *Heavenly Warriors: The Evolution of Japan's Military, 500–1300*
158. Yu-ming Shaw, *An American Missionary in China: John Leighton Stuart and Chinese-American Relations*
159. James B. Palais, *Politics and Policy in Traditional Korea*
160. Douglas Reynolds, *China, 1898–1912: The Xinzheng Revolution and Japan*
161. Roger Thompson, *China's Local Councils in the Age of Constitutional Reform*

163. Constantine Nomikos Vaporis, *Breaking Barriers: Travel and the State in Early Modern Japan*

165. James C. Baxter, *The Meiji Unification through the Lens of Ishikawa Prefecture*

166. Thomas R. H. Havens, *Architects of Affluence: The Tsutsumi Family and the Seibu-Saison Enterprises in Twentieth-Century Japan*

167. Anthony Hood Chambers, *The Secret Window: Ideal Worlds in Tanizaki's Fiction*